We pick out a text here and there to make it serve our purpose; whereas if we took all there is, and considered what went before and what followed after, we would find the text did not mean what we thought it meant.

John Seldon, 1689

Rethinking Elders

Rethinking Elders

by
Gene
Edwards

Rethinking Elders
Copyright 1998 by Gene Edwards
Printed in the United States of America
Published by The SeedSowers
            P.O.Box 285, Sargent, GA 30275

Cover design by Jenny Jeffries

Library of Congress Cataloging-in-Publication Data

Edwards, Gene
        Rethinking Elders
        ISBN 0-940232-62-6
        1. Spiritual Life.   1. Title
        Catalog Card Number:

Times New Roman 12pt

cknowledgement

To Phil Warmanen, for his assistance in correcting and proof-reading my manuscript. (If you find an error in this book, it is Phil's fault!)

*W*elcome to a new way to understand the Word of God

*V*irtually everything we are taught about the New Testament, theology and Bible teachings comes from our *use* of the Bible, rather than from the Bible.

1

Is This Any Way to Understand the New Testament?

*T*his book throws a lifeline to those of you who are suffering the consequences of the present-day concept of eldership.

But more, this book introduces to you a whole new way to study your New Testament.

The presently accepted view of elders is but one example of traditions given to us during the period of the staggering influence of Constantine (317-500 A.D.).

How far off is eldership as practiced today in comparison to the first century? As far off as are the Catholic teachings on relics, priests, nuns, pope, confessionals *and* just about every concept surrounding the clergy.

That far off? Yes, that far off.

How did we get *that* far off? We had a great deal of help! Let's first see what Luther did to us. (He too had a lot of help getting us so far off track.)

Interestingly, before Luther was a reformer, he belonged to the most mindy and philosophical branch of the Roman Catholic Church; that is, he was a student of Thomas Aquinas and Augustine.

Luther was an Augustinian monk! Augustine was a student of Aristotle, the pagan philosopher. (It has been said that Aristotle came into the Christian faith riding on the teachings of three theologians, Augustine, Thomas Aquinas and Luther. Very logical folks these four!)

Thomas Aquinas was so enamored with Aristotle's teachings that an ancient quotation emerged, "Aquinas baptized Aristotle."

For us Protestants, it was Luther who established a *way* of getting to the "truth" of the New Testament. This *way* is still *the* way we Protestants approach the New Testament to discover its teachings. It is taught in every Bible school and seminary on earth. Our present-day view of *elders* is but one case in point.

The traditional Protestant view of eldership comes to us not so much from Scripture *itself* as from the way we Protestants *approach* Scripture. Once you figure out what we are really doing, it is rather shocking to discover just how far off we got. Essentially, it goes like this: We prove our point—any point, on any subject—with a New Testament in hand, but sentence fragments on our tongues.

Virtually everything we are taught as being New Testament comes from our *use* of the Bible, rather than from the Bible.

This methodology is sometimes refered to as teaching by means of *proof text*. This approach proves *very* little, yet can "prove" anything!

This way of establishing a teaching as being "scriptural" is so prevalent and accepted in the evangelical world that it is the very blood and marrow of Protestantism. Without it, the halls of seminaries and Bible Schools might echo only silence. This approach is, at least, dangerous. This method of looking at the New Testament *prevents* us from truly seeing the first century Christians or even seeing the first century. Furthermore, it makes the Bible into something it is not—a pile of jigsaw pieces waiting for you to discover their place in a jigsaw puzzle. To illustrate:

First you select your topic. Then you pick out a series of verses from all over the Scripture, from Genesis to Revelation. Then you take the verses you have selected and arrange them in some kind of order. . .probably in an order that reinforces *your* view on your chosen subject. You then leap to logic, flavor your conclusion with rationality, and season it with traditional practices. Voila! This patchwork assemblage of sentence fragments comes together and then emerges as something that is solemnly announced to be *"absolutely the Word of God."*

Almost unnoticed, we have added very logical logic and very rational rationalization to fragments of sentences, and then invoked our conclusions as "the clear Word of God." Actually, what comes out is rarely scriptural. It is *not* the pure Word of God. This method is used to thoroughly scare just about every layman in sight into believing what he has heard.

Our entire Protestant mind-set has as its underpinnings the *proof text* approach to Scripture. *This* is scary. *Very* scary.

Just what is left out of the proof text equation? *Nearly everything!*

Words from the New Testament taken totally out of context, out of setting, and out of chronological order, then strung together, with logic as master—this, dear reader, does *not* constitute God's Word. It does not even get close.

Until you see the entire first century in an ongoing and contextual framework, until you first see the entire landscape, until you have a timeline and until that timeline is seen as a whole and set in its historical matrix, your *proof texts* have shown you *nothing*. Until Scripture is dealt with on a broad canvas, until verses are seen in their actual setting, until the ongoing chronological context is present, verse fragments show you not much more than an opinion. There is little that is accurate in the *proof text* approach to the New Testament. Prooftextism is wide open to wholesale abuse of the Scriptures, with the end result that dear brothers and sisters are hurt by these teachings disguised as instruction to "obey the Word of God."

Without first seeing the entire story, stretched out on a broad canvas, we end up with a jumbled view of everything that has to do with the Christian.

If the use of the proof text approach to the New Testament is scary, consider its origins! The proof text approach is pagan in its origins, *not* Christian.

The proof text approach to "truth" began as a servant and tool of pagan philosophers, and predates Christianity by at least 400 years. Its approach to finding truth is the very personification of rationalism, logic, and mental manipulation. This method of seeking out *truth* is Greek in origin. Its patron saint is. . .yes. . .Aristotle. He, and other Greek philosophers, raised the proof text to an art form.

This art form gave birth to yet another pagan practice we still engage in. The Greek philosophers needed to be able to quickly find the page of a book which they were arguing from (and using as a proof text), so they began dividing their favorite books into chapters and giving each sentence a number!

Yes, even our use of dividing the Bible into chapters and verses is a pagan practice predating Christianity by several hundred years, but brought over into the Christian faith in about 500 A.D. Following the heathen philosophers' example, we divided the New Testament into chapters and verses so we could argue over it better! (Just as they isolated quotations and thoughts and took those thoughts *out of* context, to thereby argue with one another more convincingly.)

Remember that, the next time you argue chapter and verse!

That which is termed "the westerner's mind" has as its very bone and marrow the use of logic (above all else) to reach its conclusions.

Behold the ancestry of proof text. All this slipped into the Christian mind-set circa 200 to 500 A.D., as natural as mother's milk.

First, *define* your topic, then follow up with *organization of thought*. This was being taught to *you* by the third grade. Aristotle is the father of "begin with a definition, follow with organized thought."

Need it be pointed out that our approach to the New Testament virtually always begins with definition and then is followed by organizing verses together. What follows next is the buttressing of our ideas by logic. You might be wise to read Aristotle's book on rhetoric to find out *how* we *Christians* study the Bible. This entire process is not so much theology as it is philosophy; however, it is usually deemed to be good New Testament theology.

Proof text theology, a blend of Aristotelian logic and the Protestant mind, garnished with sentence fragments taken from all over the Bible, this is tailor-made for being able to prove *anything* (including today's teachings and practices of eldership).

When religious men sew together a dozen Scriptures (taken from a dozen books in the New Testament) and then blend that collection into a whole, what emerges is no less than doctrine. "Biblical doctrine, truly founded on the Word of God." Well, fact is, it is not any of that.

This ancient and revered practice is not likely to *ever* go away. It will also *never* allow us to discover the Christian life as it was practiced in Century One.

The Protestant mind, and our evangelical mind which grew out of it, has *no* vehicle whatsoever for seeing the great first-century Christian saga. *It can never discover the first century.*

In fact, the very core of the protestant evangelical mind-set prohibits our seeing the first-century story. The broad canvas is *not* ours to see.

The first-century story is unknown to us.

Luther added another ingredient to this sorry mess. This ingredient guaranteed our Protestant mind would forever be jumbled up. . .and, for sure, guaranteed we would never know the first-century story. Luther gave us our *first* New Testament.

Why is *that* so tragic? It is the way he arranged the order of the New Testament books.

First, Luther continued the sacrosanct practice of making Scripture a series of numbered sentence fragments. (He took the chapter and verse idea that had been used in the Catholic Bible.)

That was nothing compared to Luther's next blow—the way he arranged Paul's epistles. This was a disaster from which we will *never* recover.

Without their chronological order, we cannot find *the story*. Paul did not write these letters in the order you find them in your New Testament. Rearrange Paul's letters in their chronological order and the first-century story emerges. And at the same time our Protestant practices take a dunking!

Now we must ask: "When did the evangelical mind begin to emerge out of the Protestant mind?" The first glimpse of the beginnings of the evangelical mind-set began around 1760, but it entered our bloodstream in the early 1800's. Enter John Darby. This man gave us the synaptics of the evangelical brain.

Here we find a true master at arranging scattered verses into grand logical teachings! Darby gave us (evangelicals) the presently accepted teachings on. . .well, just about everything we teach and practice. Including eldership.

We evangelicals rarely, if ever, get to see anything in *wholes*. We are served up a dish of fragmented thoughts, drawn together by means of logic and verses. Consequently, the end product which we are given is far, far afield from first-century reality.

(Unfortunately, the elder concept Darby gave us is not the worst thing he gave us. Among all the individual ideas he gave us, he managed to father the entire scheme of what is today known as the fundamentalist mind!)

As hard as it is for us to grasp, there really is no wisdom in extracting a verse and isolating it from an epistle, i.e. Colossians 1:7 or Ephesians 2:4.

Colossians and Ephesians are. . .*letters*. Those two letters were written by an impassioned man. But more, these two letters are part of, and fit into, a grand, sweeping story!

Dare we venture further upon this eye-opening road? If so, hold your breath as we take a turn onto a rarely travelled route. These two books not only belong to a vast sweeping story; let it also be seen these two letters were written by a church planter.

A *church planter*?

Yes.

What has that to do with anything? This: the fact that the writer was a church planter *changes* everything. This particular breed of man is virtually *extinct*. At least, the first-century version is. But without a church planter being part of the equation, everything we touch breaks down!

Paul's letters are wholes. Not a series of numbered sentence fragments. But more: The church planter is part of the story. He belongs in the equation. He is a large part of *the story*. Church planters are part of the first-century equation. Remove the church planter, and you have left out irreplaceable ingredients of New Testament Christianity and the New Testament church. Remove these and you remove any hope of knowing anything—including doctrine and practice—about Century One's version of the practice of the Christian faith.

Paul's letters are full of *the* story, and he—the travelling church planter—is a huge chunk of first-century Christianity.

Repeat: Paul's letters were written to churches. (Nine were written to churches, three to other church planters, and just one letter, *one*, to an individual. . .to a slave holder.) Place these letters in the New Testament in an order different from their chronological order, then divide these inspired letters into verses; pluck sentence fragments out of context, then rearrange them in any order that suits us—allowing us to then draw our views from *our chosen* vantage point. We end up almost annihilating the possibility of seeing the real first-century way of things.

The use of proof text (numbered verses, numbered chapters, taken from now chaotically arranged epistles, and with little knowledge of the first-century story, then blended liberally with philosophical logic) is a formula for disaster. No way can we learn Christ. . .nor the church

. . .nor anything else we call Christian if we pursue *this* course in our approach to learning the Bible.

Aristotelian logic, proof text, western rationalizing are not good tools for much of anything that has to do with the New Testament.

Nonetheless, when a man once completes his "tapestry in verse," you would be wise to not disagree with him. He may react rather poorly:

"You do not believe the clear teaching of the Word of God?" may be his reply, and who wants to have the noose of such an accusation as that tied around his neck?

Once a man—or his mentor—embraces a certain teaching arrived at by this method, it is extremely difficult for him to ever let go of it. *Fifteen* centuries of this method have convinced him that this approach *is* Scriptural. Alas, this jigsaw-puzzle approach *is* the fountainhead of our present-day practices of the Christian faith.

This book, then, is about a great deal more than eldership. It is about a better way to find what was really going on in Century One.

Eldership is but one example.

Perhaps, if we made the approach used in this book to all our teachings and practices, we would see a change in Christianity that would dwarf the Reformation.

For now, let us rescue eldership from this ancient and insidious trap.

If, in the course of this book, the thought flits across your mind that men called elders are using scare tactics, threats, proof texts, and "the clear teaching of the Word of God" as well as the threat of excommunication ("in order to help you" or "to preserve doctrinal purity" or "Christlike behavior") in your life, then perhaps another thought will flit across your mind: "Are these men *real* elders?"

Throughout its 500-year history the Protestant church has never given any great value to the *broad canvas*, to total contextuality, to *the story* in its grand continuity. But when that broad canvas is used, the present-day concept (and practice) of much of today's Protestantism falls apart. Even eldership. As we shall see.

As you read, a view of the first century may emerge that is so clear it could prove to be *very* liberating.

"Enough of verses and proof texts. There is revolution and liberation in first viewing a first-century model!"

2

Discovering Eldership, First-Century Style

*W*e shall find eldership as it really was 2000 years ago. How? By looking at the story . . .all of the story. . .the whole story.

We shall travel through that story chronologically. We shall also look at the surrounding circumstances that accompany that story. While we look we shall keep one eye on the clock, watching as it ticks off the passing of years. We shall watch the *time lapses* which took place between books in the New Testament story—and therefore we shall see the epistles in their order—and the time and circumstances which passed between books in the New Testament. . .also allowing us to see how much time, and what kind of circumstances, took place between not only the epistles but all those *verses* which we have had thrown at us!

We will take special note of the *events* which took place between those epistles, in so doing the verses may lose their present-day interpretation.

Perhaps the most explosive question we will answer as we look at elders is this: Who *ordains* elders? We seem to have forgotten to look not only at who wrote those verses, but who it was that ordained elders. Herein lies the clearest possible example of how folks who say they are teaching "only the Word of God"...*aren't!*

When using isolated verses and teaching by a method that looks very much like a jigsaw puzzle...and then when this method is laid aside and the story itself is allowed to emerge, a whole new view comes into focus. It is not unlike getting a whole new New Testament.

If the present-day teachings of eldership *were* correct, then that fact would plainly emerge from *the story itself.* The *story* would contain an eldership similar to the present-day practice of the office of elder. That does not happen.

Where it is the story versus juggling isolated verses, the story wins and the doctrine built on verses falls like a house of cards. Verses and logic must always give way to the story. You may think you have *verses* which *prove* your view of elders. Maybe you do. But *the story* will *never* agree with you. It isn't there, folks. None of it is there. *Not* in *the story.*

If today's eldership were based on the first-century story rather than on verses, then we could expect to see emerging from *the story* an eldership that would not be in control of everybody else's spiritual life. (And certainly not in control of everyone's entire life.)

On the other hand, if you overlay today's eldership and practice onto the first-century story, you would find first-century elders ordering people's lives and totally in charge of the church. (Men with verses often teach that this is the right of elders. If you hear such teaching, run for cover.)

Eldership, shepherding. . .submission and authority
. . .these teachings you may find in fragmented verses.
You will never find them in the story.

Without the story, but using only the verses, we may
be taught that elders should be in control of the meetings
of the ecclesia. We would then see the rest of God's people
in a *very* secondary role in the ecclesia, and *never* in a
leadership role. But *the story* will never show us this
scenario.

We would also expect the story to reveal to us that
virtually all church problems are handled by the elders and
only the elders. We would see elders setting the agenda
and the direction of the church. It's not there. Not in *the
story*.

We would also expect to see, in the first-century story,
elders being greatly respected, with everyone else (laymen)
giving deference to them.

In any major church crisis found in the New Testament
we should expect to see the elders front and center, and in
control. We should expect the apostles who ordained those
elders to speak directly to elders about church problems.
And the apostles' letters should be speaking to the elders
about how to handle the crisis the church is in.

The story refuses to give us such scenes.

In any major church crisis, we would expect the main
players on the stage to be the elders. It is not there. Not
in *the story*.

What you are about to read is eldership as it is found
in the drama of *the story*. To be exact, we will begin on
Sunday May 29 in the year. . .

*W*e are going to move forward through the story. . .by the clock, by the calendar, and by the contextual entirety of the story.

3

Pentecost

*S*unday, May 29, 30 A.D. When that day closed, there were only two categories of believers on this earth:

1) Twelve men who raised up a church,
and
2) Approximately 3118 other people who are referred to as *believers*.

Mark that date, 30 A.D.

No elders.

We continue on. Watch the first four chapters of Acts. These four chapters cover five or six years and record five massive influxes of new converts—perhaps more than 20,000 new converts in those five or six years.

Still no elders.

Still only two kinds of people on the stage of the first century—the *twelve* men who raised up the church in Jerusalem, and the rest. . .*the brothers and sisters.* There is no such thing as elders in the first six years of the church.

At about this time (34 A.D.) seven men are selected to wait on tables. These men have no labels. (Scripture does *not* call them deacons.) These seven men have one specific job. They are filling one specific need, the distribution of food. . .food for fifteen or twenty thousand brothers and sisters who are living in common.

You may choose to interpret that passage about these seven servers in any way you wish; just do not make these seven men elders. If you want to call them *servants*, fine; for that is what they were called in the original Greek.

It is now 36 A.D. Six years have passed since Pentecost. At this point a man named Saul of Tarsus enters the picture. Persecution rains down on the church in Jerusalem. A major crisis. How major? The church in Jerusalem ceases to exist. That means that the church in Jerusalem, over a period of six tumultuous years, with numbers which probably grew to at least 25,000 people—all living in common—still had *no* elders.

There are still only (1) God's people (seven of whom waited on tables) plus (2) the twelve men who planted the church in Jerusalem.

With persecution so severe, all the believers fled Jerusalem. Believers had vacated the city.

The Twelve now went out and began ministering in the cities, towns, and villages of Galilee and Judea where the 25,000 people fled. The Twelve became itinerant. They traveled constantly. The Twelve traveled because churches had been born in many places in Israel as a result of the massive exodus from Jerusalem.

(The people who fled Jerusalem went out and settled in towns in Galilee and Judea and as far north as Syria. These believers in each town found one another and began gathering. Suddenly there were dozens, perhaps hundreds, of smaller churches all over Israel, and even up into Syria. Persecution temporarily ended the church in Jerusalem, but it gave birth to dozens of other churches all over an entire nation. **But still *no* elders!**)

The itinerant, non-local, trans-local, extra-local, always travelling—never staying in one place—*church planters* were still on the stage. So were believers.

The kind of people who are on the stage of the story have not changed! Church planters (who are now travelling men) and God's people—that is still *all* there is.

Now we come to the year 38 A.D. The ecclesia has been upon this earth about eight years. It is safe for believers to return to Jerusalem. Some do. The Jerusalem church begins to reappear. But still no elders.

Obviously this thing of eldership was not a burning issue in those early, formative years of the ecclesia. Please note that God's people have now experienced and passed through a great deal. . .*together*. Crises upon crises. Big ones.

The people have a vast experience of taking care of the church. . .*without* elders. The *people* give direction to the church, and do so with no specific *internal* leaders. The believers look to no specific kind of leadership within. Only as leadership comes from the travelling Twelve is there any specific leadership. Any elders that might eventually emerge will have to come out of *these* people with their vast backlog of experience. They will arise out of this much history of churches existing and leading . . .without specific leaders.

We now pass through Acts until you get to Chapter Nine. It is around 38 A.D. In Acts 9 you find a new convert—one Paul of Tarsus. Paul journeyed to Jerusalem in an attempt to meet with the Twelve there. In Acts 9:27 you discover that Barnabas took Paul to the twelve apostles and introduced Paul to the Twelve. Please note, for it is very important: Barnabas presents Paul to the apostles.

There are no elders.

Then there came a time of peace to the Jerusalem church (Acts 9:31), *and* to all the churches in Judea, Galilee, and Samaria. If you read the rest of the chapter, beginning with 9:32, you will find that Peter was travelling to cities—and therefore to churches—which had sprung up all over Israel.

Still no elders.

We have only twelve travelling men and the Lord's people. We have come now to the year 40 A.D. It is *ten* years after Pentecost. Still no elders.

Continuing on through chapters 10 and 11 we finally come to Acts 11:12. Here you find a fascinating statement. Here "brothers" and "messengers," not elders, are the players in this drama.

There are brothers and sisters, in churches all over Galilee and all over Judea. There are also the apostles going about the towns and villages. The players remain only: (1) God's people (in a great many churches) and (2) twelve men ministering to these gatherings. No elders, not even *thoughts* of elders.

How did all these things work. . .without elders? Perish

the thought that churches needed only sporadic outside help and no designated internal leaders! A corporate leadership?

In Acts 11:22 the pattern continues to hold.

The word came to the attention of the Jerusalem church.

Not to apostles, and not to elders, for there are none. Word came to the church.

And they—the Jerusalem church, the brothers and sisters—sent Barnabas to Antioch.

A gathering, an assembly, *sends!*

The entire body, thousands of brothers and sisters, *send* a man out from their midst. It was a decision that was made without elders. And also made apart from the Twelve.

It is now thirteen years since Pentecost. There are probably over one hundred churches, the largest is the church in Jerusalem. Thirteen years and *still* no elders in Jerusalem.

About two or three years later, there was a famine in Jerusalem and Judea. Since there was no famine in the fledgling new church way up north in Antioch, Syria, that church sent help to the church in Jerusalem. This was accomplished even though the church in Antioch had no elders, as we shall see.

The brothers and sisters in Antioch wanted to send money to help their Jewish brothers and sisters in Judea buy food. So the Antioch Christians put together a sum of money, and then the church in Antioch selected Paul and Barnabas to go to Judea with the money. When these two men arrived in Jerusalem the church in Jerusalem was once more under *severe persecution*. The Jerusalem church is at least fourteen years old.

The record is clear; Barnabas and Paul presented the money *to the elders*!

Finally, some fourteen years after the birth of the church in Jerusalem, elders appear. Folks in the first century obviously were not in a big rush to get elders. Some fourteen years, and maybe 30,000 or more believers, does not indicate a rush to eldership.

It was at this time that Herod Agrippa (the son of Herod the Great, King over Judea, Galilee and Samaria) had James, one of the Twelve, killed. Herod also tried to find Peter and slay him. All this was going on at the time Barnabas and Paul arrived in Judea with the money. This was in April, 44 A.D. (Acts 11:19 -12:25. See specifically Acts 11:30 and also 12:25)

Now let us look at the church in Antioch. The church in Antioch began around 40 A.D., which was ten years after Pentecost. Let us watch its move along the timeline.

From its birth on, and through *all* the book of Acts, there is no indication the church in Antioch ever had elders. On the contrary, all references to the church in Antioch go out of the way to point out that the brothers and sisters in Antioch make all the decisions! Luke seems to flaunt the point that Antioch did not have elders.

By the spring of 47 A.D., which was seven years after the planting of the church in Antioch, we see that this church with no elders managed to send out two church planters. A major accomplishment for an elderless church!

Is it not true that today the tilt is toward the idea that a church cannot really manage on its own, that it must have elders?

Elders are *not* necessary. But if you try church life without elders and *also* without a church planter, you are probably doomed!

The year 47 A.D. reminds us that seventeen years have passed since Pentecost. (At this point we move from Israel and Syria to an obscure land called Galatia.)

As we do, pause for a moment. What is emerging here is a revolutionary way to study your New Testament, especially from Acts onward.

See what looking first at a chronological timeline of events does. See what happens as you look first at the story, and not isolated, chopped up, rearranged fragments (i.e. verses).

This does not just work for a study about eldership. It applies to *everything*.

Now let us look at four churches in gentile Galatia.

*I*f our present-day image of elders actually does not show up in the first century story, then our teaching and practice of eldership must be considered scripturally wrong; and therefore, this teaching and this practice ought to be abandoned.

4

Two Itinerant Church Planters in a Land Called Galatia

*I*n July of 47 A.D., seventeen years after Pentecost, Barnabas and Paul, sent out by the church in Antioch, go and preach the gospel in the lands of the heathen.

For the next *two* years Paul and Barnabas raised up four churches in Galatia. Four churches in two years, in a land where Christ had never been named.

Three of these four churches received elders within the space of less than three years. Jerusalem had elders after fourteen years. Antioch. . .never. Yet in Galatia there were three or four churches who had elders after three years. Why this great difference? We cannot know. Dare we believe. . .*variety*?

This we *do* know. Men who were itinerant church planters played the key role in bringing the very concept of eldership into existence.

These ingredients brought forth eldership:

(1) the Holy Spirit.

(2) God's people.

(3) and itinerant church planters.

You need *all three* before you can have elders. All three. Or there is *no* eldership.

What is the point? Take church planters out of the equation and you have no grounds for elders. Try to change that fact, and you will not find a single sentence (verse!) in Scripture to back you up.

Put it another way, if you have elders but there are no itinerant church planters involved, then you are *far, far* wide of the first-century mark. . .far enough to question whether those elders *are* elders.

Look at the two years Paul and Barnabas spent in Galatia. You have four churches planted, and every one of them is raised up—and then left—in a *very* short time.

Here is the amazing point: None of those churches had elders when the church planter left. There was a time lapse. . .no church planters around, no elders in the church. How can a church operate in a situation that bleak? Simple. The brothers and sisters in the ecclesia were totally in charge—no specific leader, no leaders of any kind. In this entire time the saints—only the saints—were in charge.

This means that for a good length of time, anywhere from eighteen months to a year, these churches had no leaders whatsoever, no direction from any individual or individuals, no one *in*side, no one *out*side. Later, elders were selected out from among all the people. All the people had *led* the church *before* the elders did.

"But man, proud man
Dressed in a little brief authority
Most ignorant of what he's most assured,
His glassy essence, like an angry ape
Plays such fantastic tricks before high heaven
As make the angels weep"

William Shakespeare

5

The Gentile Elders

*N*ow we come to a most amazing discovery, the establishment of elders in four very young churches in Galatia. The age of these churches: two years (Pisidia), eighteen months (Iconium), and one year (Lystra)*.

Here in Galatia, we see *quick* eldership. But there is still a gap between the *birth* of the ecclesia and (later), the choosing of *elders*. During this time frame? each church had no church planters present. And *all* leadership in the church was in the hands of God's people. A church learns how to direct before eldership arrives.

No pastor! No Bible study leaders. Just God's people. Before elders.

But that is not all we see. We see something present in those churches which is not in existence today! The *itinerant* worker is present at the selection of elders. Not a pastor. Not a local leader. From a human view the itinerant church planters, and they alone, are the one consistent influence in the decision of *who* elders will be and *when* elders will be. (Probably also *how long* those men will remain as elders.) *The itinerant workers* are the ones who lay hands on these men who are about to enter

* *There is no clear evidence that the church in Derbe had elders, but if Derbe did have elders, they were selected when the church was about eight months old.*

into eldership. No *itinerant church planters*? Then there are also no elders. Elders do not exist except in the presence of men who are itinerant workers. Not in Century One!

Without itinerant church planters the equation of eldership *collapses*, that is, if you use the *first-century* equation of eldership.

These men in Galatia who were selected as church elders came out of the brotherhood among all the men in the church. Before they were elders, all of those men were but brothers in the ecclesia. All were working together, finding direction for the church. Arising out of this context came elders. Now, the question: Do these elders, so newly appointed, become *the* leadership of the churches in Galatia? The same question could be asked of the other churches that had elders, such as the church in Jerusalem. Did *the elders* lead the church? Were they the fire brigade of all church crises?

There is solid evidence that the existence of eldership was virtually—if not totally—forgotten in Galatia during crises. You don't believe that?

Watch.

There is absolutely no evidence (or even a hint) of leadership arising from among the elders during a major crisis. A crisis which came only months after these men were appointed elders. This was one of the greatest crises of the first century. Anyone in his right mind would expect Galatian elders to come to the forefront. They didn't.

An unbelievable fact, is it not!

We would probably all agree that elders should rise and take the helm during a major crisis. Well, less than two years after those four churches received their elders, there arose a crisis in all four Galatian churches. One of church history's greatest crises! Would we not expect to see those very elders rise to the fore? And would we not expect the men (Paul and Barnabas) who planted those four churches, when writing a letter, to address the elders? And instruct them? *And also* correct these elders if they failed to act to meet the needs created by this crisis?

Don't hold your breath!

Ordinary men were picked out from among all the brothers to be these elders. Did those elders suddenly begin to run a church that had already had a strong experience of brotherhood and sisterhood?

When the crisis arose, there was no shift—the crisis belonged to all the church. To believe that elders took over a church's direction is to believe too much about eldership.

What was the duty of the Galatian elders? We do not know, but there is one thing for certain that we *do* know. There is no record—none whatsoever—that elders played any role in this catastrophic crisis which befell Galatia. It was probably the greatest crisis of the first century. The elders of Galatia were *never* players in that crisis. They existed, but the crisis—one of Moses' law versus Jesus' grace—remained wholly in the hands of (1) the apostles and (2) God's people. Let us trace the origin of the crisis and how it spread to Galatia. Let us look at *the story*.

Here is *the story*: Paul and Barnabas went to Galatia in 47 A.D. They departed Galatia two years later, returning home to Antioch, Syria (summer of 49 A.D.). They had been away from Antioch exactly two years. Keep these dates in mind as we continue.

In the meantime, a crisis was brewing. Its origins were in Jerusalem.

THE JERUSALEM - ANTIOCH CRISIS

In 50 A.D. some very legalistic Jews travelled north from Jerusalem to visit the church in Antioch. They began teaching the church in Antioch that salvation was through Christ *plus* circumcision and the law of Moses.

One church was Jewish, the other Gentile. Seemingly, the two churches were suddenly at odds. That was crisis enough. But at the same time, some of these legalistic Jewish men left Antioch and went on up to Galatia. They went up to Galatia to either get those new Gentile Christians in the four Gentile churches in Galatia to be circumcised, or to destroy those churches. Two major crises.

It's *elder* time!

The church in Jerusalem is twenty years old and has elders. The Antioch church is ten years old and has *no* elders. The four Gentile churches are between two and three years old and have elders.

The church (that is, the brothers and sisters in the Antioch church) sends an envoy to Jerusalem to see if they could straighten out the conflict between these two churches. They selected several brothers, among them Paul, Barnabas and Titus.

The *church* in Antioch sent Antioch *brothers* to:
(1) the apostles, and
(2) the elders, *and*
(3) the church in Jerusalem.

Look closely at Acts 15:2-4. The *church* in Antioch sent Barnabas, Paul, Titus and a few others to Jerusalem. This is not the action of elders, but of an entire church! The objective was for these Antioch representatives to meet with the twelve men who had planted the church in Jerusalem and with the elders of the church in Jerusalem.

Once more, it was a *church* who did the sending.

This little band of men travelled south, arrived in Jerusalem and were welcomed by. . .whom? They were welcomed *first by the church* in Jerusalem, *secondly*, by the *apostles*, and *thirdly*, by the *elders*. Read the *context*!

There were some Pharisees who did *not* welcome the Antioch delegates, because some of the Pharisees in the Jerusalem church were opposed to the Antioch church's lack of circumcision.

Remember, at this same time a group of Jewish legalists were in Galatia, trying to force the four young churches to obey Jewish customs. "If you are not circumcized, you are not saved" was the message these new Gentile Christians in Galatia were hearing. And the message was coming to them from the mother church in Jerusalem.

Let us consider this scene. According to all that you

have heard on eldership you would probably think that the elders up in Galatia would be rising up to protect the church from these Jerusalem Judaizers.

A few men from Antioch sat down in a room in Jerusalem with (1) twelve church planters, and (2) the elders of the Jerusalem church. (There have been elders in Jerusalem for *only* six years.) Somewhere between twenty and thirty men were in that room. Look carefully at the situation. As in the entire sweep of the first-century story, the elders in that room were linked to the men who had *planted* that church.

Representatives from both churches debated for several days. A final decision was made by Peter and James, *not* by elders.

This final decision was made by Peter and James, *not* by elders.

This decision pleased (1) the Twelve, and then (2) the elders. But never forget this decision also pleased (3) the entire church in Jerusalem. (Acts 15:22) That was a church imprinted with a strong history of *everyone* functioning and everyone involved.

It was an entire church which sent the men from Antioch back to Antioch. . .and it was an *entire* church in Jerusalem which blessed the Antioch/Jerusalem decision.

Now comes another decision from Jerusalem. They decide to send some representatives from Jerusalem to travel up to Antioch and, upon arrival, to tell the Antioch church all that took place in Jerusalem while Paul and Barnabas were there. Who made the decision to send this

Jerusalem envoy to Antioch? It took the apostles, the elders, *and the Lord's people* to make this decision.

So, a few Jerusalem believers went with Barnabas, Paul, and Titus back to Antioch carrying a Jerusalem letter that was written to Antioch.

Read Acts 15:23.

Those of you who see a broad mantle for eldership please take note. The letter begins *"the apostles,"* next it says *"the brothers,"* and finally it says *"the elders."*

Once more you find three kinds of people at the center of the stage of the first century: church planters, brothers and sisters and. . .*sometimes*. . .elders.

Again, note the inseparable link of the apostles with eldership.

But that is Jerusalem, the *sender*. What of Antioch, the *receiver*? Look how Jerusalem addresses its letter to the church in Antioch. The momentous, historical letter begins:

"To the *brothers* in Antioch."

It is the Lord's people, the Twelve, and elders who send the letter. It is *the brothers* who *receive* the letter. And the Jerusalem visitors who, while they visited Antioch, "strengthened the *brothers and sisters* in Antioch." (15:32)

In Jerusalem there are *three* kinds of people. But within Antioch (a church that is ten years old) there are no elders, only brothers.

(Acts 15 is the last reference in Acts to elders until you come to Acts 20:18. These five chapters traverse a period of eight years.) There is a great deal of storm, fury, crisis, and chaos which takes place during those eight years, yet no sense that elders were in any way involved. . .not in leadership, nor in solutions.

*T*he office of the elder is inexorably linked to that of the non-local church planter. Remove the element of the church planter and you remove true eldership. True eldership exists only where itinerant church planters also exist. To try to create an eldership among God's people by any other means does violence to the Scripture. . .and to God's people.

6

The Galatian Story

*T*he brothers from Jerusalem came to visit the church in Antioch not knowing that at that very moment a far greater crisis was at its peak up in Galatia.

The Judaizers who have travelled to Galatia intended to circumcise the brothers in the four churches or destroy the four churches. Yes, it is very definitely time for elders! And these four churches do *have* elders.

Those Jerusalem Judaizers, now in Galatia, did not know of the decision that had been made in Jerusalem. And down in Antioch and down in Jerusalem, neither Paul and Barnabas nor the Twelve had any knowledge of those Judaizers up in Galatia. When Paul did learn of their presence and the destruction they were causing, he sat down and wrote the first piece of Christian literature ever penned. We call it the book of *Galatians*.

The letter we call *The Book* of Galatians is six pages long (or should we say six pages *short*).

Remember this letter is written to four churches—all young, all Gentile. These are churches composed of ex-heathen; churches which are somewhere between two-and-a-half years old to perhaps four years old. All have elders

(Acts 14:23). Oh, but those four churches also had *brothers and sisters.*

Antioch is handling this crisis without elders. Jerusalem is handling the crisis with church planters and elders. But what of Galatia? Galatia had elders (and no church planter present). Who handled the Galatian crisis?

Remember, as Paul put pen to parchment these four churches are in crisis and chaos. Some believers have surrendered to being circumcised. Some are even obeying the Sabbath and following the Jewish calendar of moons and festivals! On the other hand, some have refused to be circumcised. Confusion reigned everywhere.

In the midst of all this, does Paul think of *elders*? Does he think: write the elders? He ought to. (I would!)

Or does he think: brothers and sisters?

The letter Paul wrote to those four churches reveals the inner workings of an ecclesia in the first century. Perhaps it reveals true church life. . .a way of life we are not capable of imagining. That letter also helps us see clearly the lost office of a church planter.

Whenever Paul thought in terms of those men who were supposed to be "in charge" during this crisis, he thought of brothers and sisters. Read the letter. In the presence of all that carnage, not once do elders enter Paul's mind. You have never seen a church in a greater crisis. Neither have I. None of us ever will. Nonetheless, Paul did not turn to elders as a source of help in solving this crisis.

Accept the present-day teaching about elders and you

are compelled to believe that if the eldership did not step into this crisis and deal with it, they certainly should have. They should perhaps even deal with the crisis in a swift, calculated and confrontational way. (Such conduct has been known to happen in our day, in far *smaller* crises.) Perhaps the elders should even throw some people out of the ecclesia?

All sorts of discipline? All sorts of excommunications? All sorts of orders, commands? Wall to wall authority?

It is not there! Not in the story of Galatians. Such practices, such ideas, did not exist! Consider *that* fact and you are forced to *re*consider traditional teaching about eldership!!

Here is reality.

The only person from any of the Galatian churches who stepped into that crisis was a young kid from Lystra. He was somewhere between the ages of seventeen and twenty one (and a *future* church planter in Galatia). It was not "elders to the rescue," but a *boy*.

Paul sent his letter to Galatia.

Then he and Silas set out from Antioch to Galatia. These two men—church planters—came to the churches in Galatia to clean up the crisis there. In recording this story, neither Acts nor Galatians mentions *elders*. Once more, please observe that the only people on the stage are (1) the two church planters, and (2) the brothers and sisters, plus a half-breed kid (half Jewish and half Gentile) named Timothy. Timothy was the one person who stepped into the fray and did something. We do not know what it was that Timothy did, but *whatever* it was, it impressed *everyone,* including men much older than Timothy.

Does Acts 6:1 read *"and elders in the four churches commended Timothy?"* No. There is no such mentality working here. The record says *"the brothers and sisters* spoke highly" of young Timothy. Here again we are allowed a window into the soul of the first-century church. We see her mind-set. No "elder thinking" here. But lots of "the brothers and sisters."

The only other person to step into the crisis? A church planter!

If you are one who teaches eldership a la Luther, Calvin, and especially Darby, please explain the absence of any reference to elders or overseers in the letter to the Galatians.

Now let us take a close look at this letter which Paul wrote to Galatia. By any measure of what you and I have been taught about elders, that book (a scorchingly hot letter written in anger) should start off by saying ". . .to the elders in Galatia. . ." or ". . .to the brothers and sisters, and to the elders. . . ."

Read the letter. Turn that letter upside down. Turn it on its edge. Read it upside down, read it sideways, read it from bottom to top, read it backwards. Read it in Greek or in Latin or in hieroglyphics. Read it along the edges of the sheet. Read it anyway you desire, and you cannot find one single iota of an idea, thought, insinuation or implication that elders existed in those four churches.

Elders *did* exist in those churches. Nonetheless, in

this chaotic situation an "elder thought" did not exist. Why? Because we have misunderstood what elders are. In a crisis it was a young kid from Lystra named Timothy, and it was *the churches* themselves who rode out that storm. . .and triumphed! The center of the church was not dominated by elders, or pastors, or deacons. The central activity of the church emanated from its true center, the brothers and sisters. And *they* triumphed over those Jewish proselytizers!

Those of you who demand submission to elders, those of you who have crushed God's people in mini-crises, those of you who have divided churches, excommunicated folks, and have pontificated about the importance and sanctity of an elder. . .deal with this! All evidence points one way: The churches of the first century were led by brothers and sisters, not elders!

"But if elders don't deal with a crisis, who does?"

The answer is simple and it is obvious!

The man most needed, but the man nobody wants, *the church planter*.

Who else?

A people—God's people—the *brothers and sisters* who have, *beforehand,* led the church.

The stage will not yield. The main players on the stage of the first century are still God's people and itinerant church planters.

You will never, never be in a church that was in a greater crisis than these four were. Yet you bring elders to the front. You discipline and hurt God's people. You rebuke them. You order them around. Why? Because you are having some sort of a crisis, discomfort, or threat to *your* position, to *your* title, and *your* authority. Cheap Christianity, sir. Very cheap Christianity.

The only reason you can get away with this kind of conduct is because you do not have an itinerant church planter. (Church planters were the champions of the believers, not their executors.) Such men would STOP your conduct cold! You only get away with this brazen, bizarre conduct because you have a title. That title is worthless if it was not bestowed on you (1) by an itinerant—non-local—church planter. . .and (2) God's people. You have no right to exist in a position of eldership outside those two ingredients.

Be an elder, have that position, hold that title—if you dare. But know this: You did not get your position by any means known to first-century believers.*

We are now in the late summer of 50 A.D.

It has been twenty years since Pentecost. There is only one piece of Christian literature in existence (the book of Galatians). Paul and Silas are in Galatia, but only for a few days. After that, the church planters *left* Galatia. Itinerant church planters have a habit of doing that. The Galatian churches had been in a crisis for several months, yet Paul visited these churches for maybe two weeks . . .and then left them all on their own. . .again! Furthermore, Paul and Silas stole away from those four churches the only decent helper they had locally. They

I invite you to write a pamphlet explaining why elders were not mentioned in any of the crises occurring in any of the Gentile churches. I do not know what your reasoning will be, but you had better be prepared to come up with some amazing stuff, because the next six letters Paul pens—like the one penned to the churches in Galatia—make no mention of elders. Be sure to explain that, too.

took Timothy! Then they left Galatia and went over to Europe!

Please note that we are faced once more with travelling, itinerant, extra-local, non-local, trans-local brothers who plant churches and then get up and leave those churches while the churches are in their infancy! If you ever wondered just how simple brothers and sisters could so effectively lead the church, without books, buildings, or Bibles, the answer is easy: They got left on their own to sink or swim! They learn to lead fast. In the Protestant era we *never* dare do such a thing. And voila! God's people never learn to lead.

We go now to Europe.

Paul, Silas, and Timothy enter the city of Philippi in Northern Greece. It is late summer of 50 A.D.

*I*f church planters do not exist in our dispensation, where is the verse that says their role and responsibility moves into the hands of elders or pastors? Where does the New Testament teach that the non-local church planter ceases to exist and all his office goes into the hands of local leaders?
We cannot forfeit the role of church planters without creating Scriptural chaos!
Their role in the church is indelible and irrevocable.

7

A Crisis Among the Greeks

e learned a great deal from the saints in Syria and from four churches in Galatia. The timeline goes on, the story continues to unfold.

The calendar and clock tick off the passing of days and months. And a whole new view of Christianity continues to open before us. How clear things become when we cease to deal with scattered sentence fragments! We now come to Philippi, Greece, in Europe. We will again see four Gentile churches. All four are Greek churches in the land of the Greeks. Like the four churches in Galatia, they have much to teach us.

Paul and Silas raised up a church in Philippi in northern Greece. The two church planters were in the city of Philippi for a total of four months (circa August - December of 50 A.D.). (Acts 16:12)

Mark this! Some thirteen years after Paul came to Philippi, he wrote a letter to the church in Philippi. We call that letter the book of *Philippians*.

Thirteen years after the church in Philippi was born, it got a letter from Paul! Keep that in mind as we will come back to this fact later.

From a Roman prison in 63 A.D. Paul wrote to the ecclesia in Philippi. In that letter, only in that letter, did Paul ever refer to elders. (Paul wrote nine letters to churches. He mentioned elders in only one of those nine letters.)

A church in northern Greece is raised up by an itinerant church planter in 50 A.D. That church planter then left that young church, just four months later. No elders. Why? Pick your reason, but here is the best one: Paul was suddenly and unexpectedly ordered out of the city.

A "brothers and sisters" mentality *and* practice emerged. Not an "elders" mentality. That brothers and sisters way of thinking, acting, and behaving dominates all the churches in all the ensuing years. In each church born in Greece, a strong brotherhood and a strong sisterhood arise in the early stages.

Philippi is one of only five churches in all the New Testament that we know had elders. Jerusalem, three churches in Galatia, Philippi and Ephesus, with churches on the island of Crete *about* to get elders.

Philippi probably did not have elders for at least a decade—long enough for a brother and sister outlook and practice to pervade that entire church. Whenever it was that Philippi got elders, one fact is certain; those elders emerged out of a strong brotherhood which *preceded* eldership. Elders on the premises does not mean that a strong brotherhood suddenly dissolves, with all power going into the hands of the elders. This matter of brotherhood preceding elders is consistent throughout the story. Elders taking precedence over the brotherhood never happened. Not in Century One.

Paul and Silas have now planted one church in Europe. They left, having been in Philippi less than six months. Time ticks, the calendar moves, and we are watching a matrix, a chronological model of eldership emerging . . .not a "sentence fragment," "patchwork," "proof text" model, but a totalistic, contextual model.

Paul and Silas move on to Thessalonica (Acts 17:1). They will be there from January to May of 51 A.D.

It is only for a total of four months that the two men are in Thessalonica. Thessalonica is left on its own. No elders.*

Leaving Thessalonica, the two men arrive in Berea in June 51 A.D. There Paul and Silas raise up a church. They were in Berea about four months. Then, as in all other places, the two men departed a church only four months old. As in Philippi, their departure was sudden and unplanned. There is virtually no chance of elders being selected.

After Paul and Silas left Berea, Paul made a short stop in Athens (Acts 17:16). Paul spent October and November travelling to Athens, staying there briefly and then travelling on to a city in southern Greece called Corinth.

Paul arrived in Corinth in November of 51 A.D.

How old is the church in Thessalonica when Paul arrives in Corinth? It is about eight or nine months old.

At the time Paul entered Corinth (late 51 A.D.), he wrote a letter back to the ecclesia in Thessalonica. That

*About four or five months after Paul left Thessalonica he wrote a letter to this nine-month-old Thessalonican church. We call that letter I Thessalonians (Acts 17:10).

letter is the second piece of Christian literature ever penned. Remember, the church was no more than nine months old when it received Paul's letter. Why this letter?

Because the Thessalonian church was in a major crisis, the kind of crisis for which elders are tailor-made.

*L*et all teaching about the New Testament
begin first with a complete model of the
first century

8

Another Letter to a
Church in Crisis

*I*f Thessalonica had elders, Paul certainly forgot that fact while writing First Thessalonians.

With elders, and from our present view of elders, we would expect this letter to begin ". . .*to the elders in Thessalonica. You elders get these problems straightened out!*" Or perhaps Paul might be expected to have written ". . .*to the brothers and sisters, in the church in Thessalonica, and to the elders. . . .*"

The church was in a terrible state. How terrible? A lot bigger than crises churches have today when they call out the elders and heads begin to roll. People had quit working. They were expecting the Lord to come back any minute. Others in the church were having to support those who had stopped working. There was confusion about some believers who had recently died. There was even someone perpetrating the idea that there was no resurrection. (Doctrinal heresy of the worst sort! Roll out the elders!)

Listen to how Paul *really* begins his letter: "Paul and Silas and Timothy to the church in Thessalonica which is in God the Father and the Lord Jesus Christ. Grace. . ."

He begins by thanking God for all of them. The word *brothers* appears in this letter *fourteen times*. References to Jesus Christ abound. References to God the Father abound. References to the church abound. References to the problems abound.

But there is not one whisper of anything that would indicate elders. No submission and authority to elders. Not one mention of elders! Elders are not there.* To whom then does Paul give responsibility to work out Thessalonian problems? To the brothers and sisters. (1 Thess. 5:14)

The responsibility of handling a crisis falls upon the ecclesia. Why? Because the ecclesia can handle it. (With a little non-local nudge.)

The church in Thessalonica had been in existence nine months. In that time it had gone through severe persecution and then chaos. Locally, who is at the helm?

Nobody except the brothers and sisters.

Read the letter.

Paul's mentality—his whole process of thinking—his memory banks, the engrams and synapses of his brain waves—do not contain an *elders* thought! He has a *brothers* mentality. May God give us back such a pattern of thinking! If we *do* regain that way of thinking, it will be because we live in a community of believers who live this way.

God hasten the day!

The church in Thessalonica has a lesson to show us. We continue on through Century One.

What of I Thessalonians 5:12? This is a reference to Silas and Timothy, not to anyone else.

You are seeing a chronological, matrix-centered *model.* Compare that model with the proof text approach. Which rings clear? Now we travel on to southern Greece, and to Corinth. If ever a church needed elders. . .

I sit on a man's back, choking him and making him carry me, and yet assure myself that I feel very sorry for him and wish to lighten his load by all possible means—except getting off his back.

Tolstoi

9

A Second Letter to
that Church in Crisis

*S*ome three months after Paul wrote
I Thessalonians he wrote a second letter to
Thessalonica. More problems. More crises.

In Paul's second epistle to Thessalonica, he still makes
no mention of elders. This book, too, speaks of Jesus
Christ. . .of God the Father. . .of brothers and sisters. . .of
the church.

This is where Paul's thoughts are. It seems that this is
where Paul's thoughts *always* are.

If we grant that there were elders in the church in
Thessalonica, there is not a hint that he expected elders to
do anything.

Remember also, a church planter wrote these two
letters. . .and a church planter—an *outside* church
planter—is the one who handled this crisis. This is as it
should be, first-century style.

Now observe the content of the letter. You see the
problems, but do you see the doctrine of eldership being
taught? In the *nine* letters Paul wrote to churches, he
never taught anything about eldership.

(The practice of sewing verses together to find out
"what the Bible says" is beginning to fall apart. Be assured

we have only *begun* to see our much venerated teaching of eldership fall apart.)

If you wish to say that the church in Thessalonica had no elders, then you again have a *brotherhood* and *sisterhood* which took care of all the church's problems. If you say there were no elders in Thessalonica until later, you also acknowledge that elders eventually emerged out of an incredibly strong brotherhood. A brotherhood tested by fire! Such a brotherhood is not likely to suddenly turn all leadership, direction, *and* meetings over to elders. It is not only leadership which today's elders have; they also control the meetings themselves. In Century One, there was no such practice. . .nor even such a thought!

Paul is now in Corinth. It is late 51 A.D. Paul will raise up a church in Corinth and remain in that city for a total of eighteen months.

He worked with the church in Corinth for one-and-a-half years. This is a longevity record. *(All* the previous churches got only four to six months of Paul's presence among them.)

Would you like to be a member of a church with that short a time for a foundation, that brief a period of help, and then be left on your own?

Five more years will pass before Paul again writes a letter to a church. He will be in Ephesus when he writes that letter. Ironically, the letter will be written to Corinth! The church in Corinth will be seven years old. . .and it will *not* have elders! Corinth will be a church in great crisis. If there are no elders after seven years, who in the world is driving the bus?

*E*xplain your doctrine by your life

Matthew Pryer

10

The Crisis in Corinth
and the Role the Elders Played
in that Crisis

*P*aul arrived in Corinth in November 51 A.D. He wrote them a letter six years later while he was living in Ephesus.

You must answer for yourself this question. During those six years did the church in Corinth get elders?

Remember, Paul had not written a letter to any church in at least six years, yet a great deal happened during those intervening years.

Paul had departed Corinth after being with the church there for eighteen months, and he went down to Jerusalem. From Jerusalem he returned to his home in Antioch, Syria. It was while in Antioch that Paul made the most extensive preparation for a journey that he had ever made. After about a year of preparation for that third journey, Paul left Antioch and headed out for new territory—Ephesus, in Asia Minor.

Paul arrived in Ephesus in the summer of 54 A.D. He spent three years in Ephesus. In June of 57 A.D.—some six years after Paul had started the church in Corinth—he received some very disturbing news from Corinth. It was this news which provoked Paul to write First and Second Corinthians.

It would take several pages for you and me to *list* the problems the church in Corinth was having. Simply stated, the church in Corinth was on the verge of a split. Paul genuinely feared that the church *would* split. He also feared that the church in Corinth might reject him in totality. When Paul sat down to write I Corinthians he feared that his letter might literally destroy the church and end his relationship to it.

(In II Corinthians Paul tells the brothers and sisters in Corinth just how much he had feared that these very things might happen. See II Corinthians Chapter 1.)

If ever there was an ecclesia in the first Christian century that was in the middle of a disaster, it was the church in Corinth. If ever there was a church that needed elders, we would all agree that it was the church in Corinth.

There were people getting drunk at the Lord's Supper, while others were getting nothing to eat. There was incest, and worse, nobody was doing anything about correcting it. The church itself was divided into three or four camps: The Peterian camp, the Apollonian camp, the Paulinian camp, and the we-are-above-this-situation camp. Beyond that, the meetings were wild and completely out of control. *Surely*, it is "elder time"!

Now read I Corinthians. Can you find any reference to elders?

Any body of believers which meets outside the traditional way churches meet, and which has elders, facing a situation similar to this, would find elders "eldering" all over the place. Yet in all this letter, there is not even a hint of Paul's speaking to anyone in this letter, except as he addressed the brothers and sisters. From start to finish, he addressed the entire church. Only the entire church. Such was the Christian world he knew and lived in. In Paul's mind, there was simply no one else to address.

It is difficult for any of us today to understand how Paul would not call upon some element of leadership in the church to bring things into order. . .or, at least, out of chaos.

There is no indication of elders in Corinth. There is no addressing of the problems, except to the *entire* church. There is a very important element at work here, one which simply does not exist today.*

Once more, consider the presence of the itinerant church planter. We seem to be determined *not* to return to the itinerant church planter. These men were the ones who helped take care of the situation in Corinth. *Not* elders, but travelling church planters. First, the brothers and sisters themselves; and secondly, the brother who wrote the letter to Corinth. The solution lay only with them. In fact, except for the brothers and sisters, only three men played a role in straightening out the Corinthian mess. One was Timothy, one was Titus, and the other was Paul. All three of those men were itinerant church planters.

We come back to the same unmovable fact. That fact will not change, it will not budge. The church planter and the church are inseparably linked. The church planter and elders are inseparably linked. If you remove the role of the itinerant, outside, non-local church planter from the

---

One of these days I hope to publish a book entitled **The Man Most Needed But the Man Nobody Wants** *to more fully address the issue of our needing to return to the practice of having itinerant church planters.*

first-century ecclesia, eldership disappears.

True eldership exists only with the existence of the itinerant church planter. And church problems are resolved by (1) God's people and (2) the church planter.

Strange, is it not, that for seventeen centuries we have been very busy centering on elders? Yet in that same period of time—and certainly now, with our current mind-set—not a peep do we hear concerning the role of church planters.

Why?

If you read the letter again you will see that Paul of Tarsus—the man responsible for the existence of that church and also a man *not* local to that church—took full responsibility for everything going on in Corinth. He inserted himself right in the middle of the mess and began solving the problems. He never addressed any specific leaders; it was *Paul* and *the church* who would work these problems out.

Those of you who teach a *strong* eldership, will you explain why there is no reference to elders in I Corinthians or II Corinthians? If ever your doctrine of elders needed to be front and center on the stage of ecclesiology, then it would be right here. Why, too, do men so enamored with employing elders run from the idea of a non-local church planter as though the very thought of such a notion would bring back the plague of the Black Death?

References in the New Testament to Christian elders? Seventeen. References to church planters? Close to a thousand!

You *are* teaching us "the pure Word of God" regarding elders?

Let us all flee men who know the Bible well enough to paint the planet with the doctrine of eldership, while, at the same time never mentioning the possibility that truly we need the church planter far more than we need elders.

Paul's letters to Corinth were well received. He soon left Ephesus and came again to Corinth. And while there in Corinth, our brother Paul wrote yet another letter—his greatest letter. That letter can teach us a great deal about elders. The name of this letter is. . .

*H*eed the words of the Trojans:
Beware the teacher bearing
verses!

11

The Letter to the Romans

*I*n the winter of 57 A.D. or early 58 A.D. while Paul was visiting the church in Corinth, he wrote to the ecclesia in the city of Rome.

Rome was farther away from Paul, in distance, than was any other city to whom he ever wrote a letter.

This church, the church in Rome, had been well founded. Still, you can search that letter forever and you will not find a single mention of elders. The matrix of Paul's mind is still. . .brothers and sisters.

There is no crisis going on in the church in Rome, but the letter, by its very nature, was a wonderful place to discuss eldership. Here was a church he had never seen, but a church which he felt responsible for. . .just as those living in Rome felt connected to him. It was a sweeping letter, one instructive on the entire Christian landscape, but no mention of the place of eldership in the church.

We now have six letters to churches. Six letters in which Paul does not mention elders. Six letters to a total of seven churches, *with no mention of elders.

This is especially mystifying when it comes to the letter to the ecclesia in Rome. Paul, now rather old, is drawing

The six churches are: Pisidia, Iconium, Lystra, Derbe, Thessalonica, Corinth, and now Rome.

on all his past experience in writing to this young church. He is reaching out to help them in all future situations they may pass through. All of chapters 12-16 are about church life with all its problems and pitfalls. Yet, during all his past experience with churches and crises in churches, nothing comes to mind about eldership!

Only one thing can be concluded, and it is this: The thought of eldership was not utmost in Paul's mind, ever.

In the midst of terrible, unbelievable, almost unimaginable crises in the four churches in Galatia, the crisis in the church in Thessalonica, and the truly disastrous situation in Corinth, Paul relates to each of those churches as though the problems rest wholly between all the brothers and sisters in the church. . .and himself.

This is the way Paul always saw things. Paul was personally responsible to the church. The church as a whole was responsible for leadership, responsible for the direction the church took, responsible for how the meetings developed, and responsible for working with Paul in times of crisis.

Lord, give us back such a day.

Paul was an itinerant church planter. Paul was *not* a home Bible teacher, he was not a pastor, nor was he a "head elder." Eldership among the Paulinian churches simply did not loom large in anyone's thinking. That was because eldership did not loom large in the church practices. If you understand that elders come out of a *strong* brotherhood, then this is not an odd concept. But on the other hand, if you follow today's teaching on eldership, even though you may continue to preach the priesthood and function of all believers, you can say good-bye to any hope of having the priesthood and function of believers or outside workers.

Today's elders would be among the last people on earth to ever propose the return of the itinerant church planter. They know that in one fell swoop the present practice of eldership would tumble like a house of feathers.

Probably most of the churches Paul planted did not have elders. At least three churches in Galatia did; yet even there, eldership did not come until after a period of time when everyone was involved in the church's life and direction. When the church in Corinth was at least six years old, it did not have elders. The church in Thessalonica was young, as were the churches in Galatia; but Thessalonica, unlike Galatia, had no elders. *And* in every case, eldership and church planter are inexorably entwined.

Now, as we continue on through the story, we come to a very clear example of elders.

henever a man has cast a longing eye on offices, a rottenness begins in his conduct.

Jefferson

12

The Elders in Ephesus

*P*aul was in Ephesus three years. As we have seen, Paul was in Ephesus when he wrote I Corinthians and II Corinthians.

At some point Paul appointed elders in Ephesus. When? During those three years? More likely, about the time he departed from Ephesus. No question about it, no *if*'s, no *and*'s, no *but*'s, at some point Paul appointed elders in Ephesus.

Here again, we see an inconsistency. There is *no* pattern as relates to churches having elders or not having elders. Antioch seemed to have no elders. Philippi seemed to have no elders early on. Thessalonica had no elders. Berea has no mention of elders. Certainly, if Corinth had elders they did the best job of hiding that one can imagine.

Now here is the church in Ephesus with elders. But exactly when these men were selected as elders we do not know.

We know that Paul's time in Ephesus ended because of a riot there. Just before he left, it appears that Paul gathered in all the believers in Ephesus and exhorted them. Then he departed. This was in about March of 58 A.D.

This departure ended the longest stay Paul ever spent in a church: three years. After Paul walked out of the city of Ephesus, he made a one-hundred-mile trip across the Aegean Sea to Greece. Scholars agree that while there he visited all four of the Greek churches. First he visited the three ecclesiae in northern Greece: Philippi, Thessalonica and Berea. Then he travelled on down to southern Greece and visited the ecclesia in Corinth. Paul stayed in Corinth for about three months. (While there he wrote Romans.) Paul then went back to northern Greece. Leaving Greece by sea he went as close to Ephesus as he dared.

Why not revisit Ephesus?

Paul had discovered that a group of Jewish zealots called *daggermen* had made a vow to kill him. It was a vow unto death: that is, they would not eat or drink until they had killed Paul; death alone would end the vow to kill him.

A foreboding spirit spread over the churches, a sense that Paul did not have much longer to live.

Here is what happened. Leaving Greece by sea, Paul decided to send the young men who were with him to the city of Troas. Paul left southern Greece alone, returning quickly to northern Greece, while his friends set sail directly to Troas in Asia Minor. Paul went first to Philippi. He then sailed to Troas.

Paul had visited as many of the churches as he possibly could before going on to Jerusalem.

(It was in Troas that Paul spoke so late that someone sitting on the window sill fell asleep and fell out the third story window.)

Leaving Troas, Paul walked to a city called Assos. (His friends sailed, probably to confuse anyone trying to follow Paul.) In Assos, Paul joined his friends. From Assos they all took a ship sailing to a city called Mitylene, from that city he went on to Samos, and from Samos to Miletus. When he reached Miletus he was near Ephesus, but he dared not go there. Also he was running out of time. He was determined to get to Jerusalem for the Passover.

(Paul was hoping that once he reached Jerusalem, he could allay the fears of the Jerusalem Jews about his reverence for the Law of Moses.)

All along the way, Christians—and churches—were warning Paul that going to Jerusalem might cost him his life. Still, Paul determined to go, as the church in Jerusalem was once again divided over him. Paul was willing to lay down his life to preserve the unity between the Jewish churches and the Gentile churches.

In the midst of all this drama, Paul—not able to get to Ephesus—sent word asking the elders of the church in Ephesus to come visit him in the city of Miletus.

Luke tells us what happened. To read the passage is to grasp a little of the tension, fear, crisis and danger which filled the air. The record of Paul's visit with the Ephesian elders is one of the most passionate, moving passages in all Scripture.

Those who teach a strong, pervasive eldership base a great deal of their teaching on this passage.

You might wish to read Acts 20:22-35. Note: This is a total of *thirteen* verses.

The first six verses in this passage are a beautiful statement from Paul about his way of life as he walked among the churches. He specifically talks to the elders about his manner of living while he dwelt in Ephesus for those three years. He breaks the hearts of the dear brothers listening to him, telling them that he would never see their faces again. (Paul was wrong—he did make it back to Ephesus.)

Paul is *not* discussing *eldership* in this passage. What he is saying is that he had lived a blameless life before God's people and before the church. Why did he say these things? Simple. He wanted those elders to be as patient and compassionate as he was. Paul raised a standard for elders to live by. He tells them of his forebearance, how he worked among them, how he never took money—not for anything—ever! He reminded them of his tenderness and his patience. (He worked night and day among them— he was not a full-time minister. He made his own living, making no money off the churches.)

All this passage is full of broad hints of how an elder should walk. High standards indeed! These are five of the thirteen verses—what of the next eight sentences?

Only in four verses (28, 29, 30 and 31) does Paul address eldership. Out of these thirteen emotionally packed sentences Paul's actual *instructions* to the elders are in only *two* verses.

What is Paul saying to these elders, beyond reminding them of *his own* compassion, his own caring, his own tenderness, his aloofness from money, his patience in forbearing?

With all the strong emphasis on the conduct of elders, please, you who would be elders, concentrate not so much on those two instructive verses, but on the example of Paul's own life. Remember the *way* he walked in the midst of the church. Very few men who have borne the name elder—and who have used that office in the way it has been taught in our day—would be able to reach the incredibly noble ground exemplified by Paul's life. In fact, Paul stood in front of those elders, and *mostly* said, "*Look at my own life.*"

Who chose those elders? Well, we assume the church did, and that the Holy Spirit did. There is one thing for certain, there was an itinerant church planter present in the church in Ephesus when those men were selected; and when he spoke, they listened. This same man was admonishing those same men to repeat his life, his lifestyle, his manner and his standard.

Please note that these elders were not selected by a pastor, because the pastor as we know him was not invented until the time of Martin Luther. Paul was not a pastor. Neither was he a Bible teacher who had gathered a group of people together for Bible study in someone's living room. Neither was he one of the elders in Ephesus. This was a travelling man, as were all the other church planters in the first century.

Once more you are forced to face the fact that there is no justification for the existence of elders outside of a relationship to an itinerant church planter.

Now, let's look at those words of instruction: "Guard yourself."

To anyone who might become an elder, first-century style, your first guarding is to guard *yourself*. *Next* you guard the flock.

"Guard yourself." How? Perhaps to be not proud of your responsibilities. Guard, to not "throw your weight around." Guard, not to hurt others.

Paul then says, "the Holy Spirit has appointed you to be *watchers*." A shepherd watches the flock. As a shepherd watches the flock, so elders watch the church of God.

Then Paul reminded them that elders are a small thing in the greater picture. Jesus Christ shed His blood for the church of God, emptied Himself for her.

"*You* love her and *you* lay down your life for *her*." (You do not become a dictator over her.)

Why are these men to watch? What are they watching for? Externally, they are watching for a man who has dogged the path of Paul throughout most of Paul's ministry. This man has vowed to go to any Gentile church Paul raises up and either bring that church under Mosaic law or destroy that church. This man is Paul's "thorn in the flesh." Watch for *him*.

So, on the *outside*, keep a look out for. . .

Legalists!

Well, that particular man is now dead. But legalists and legalism are not dead.

Once more, Paul speaks of his own life. The men whom Paul is warning are men who have not always been elders. They had watched Paul's life for three years when they were but brothers without designation. Nor is Paul speaking only to the elders in this passage. His words are meant for all the brothers and sister in Ephesus. He is reminding the entire church in Ephesus: "Remember how I lived." And "watch."

Paul of Tarsus did not act the way many of today's elders act. He lived free of church money. He exhorted; he did not order. He warned, but when he warned, his face was covered with tears. He took no money, and he had compassion. He worked with his own hands. He paid for his own meals and his own board and room. And he took no money. He was a passer-through, a sojourner, an itinerant worker. And he took no money.

God give us such men!

Search this "elder passage" for practical advice on the "how" of being an elder. The main thing was to watch and to guard, to warn and to prepare.

We will return to this passage a little later on, there to find a real shocker—something incredibly overlooked.

Just a few years after this incident, these very elders were brought in front of all the brothers and sisters and publicly rebuked for misusing the office. *These* very men! (Guess who did the rebuking.)

In another book which Paul of Tarsus wrote, he referred to these very elders. You will find this in the book called I Timothy. Later on, when you and I come to the book of I Timothy, we will explore further. So let us remember this dramatic scene.

Later Paul, the itinerant church planter, will talk to

Timothy, the itinerant church planter, about *the elders in Ephesus*. Paul's words to Timothy may blow your "elderology."

Before making a strong case for an overlordship of men called elders (a doctrine extracted from this passage), please read the context of that beautiful passage.

Paul, in a passage in I Corinthians, addressing the royal mess there, refers to himself as a *mother* and as a *father*.

As you remember motherhood and fatherhood, remember Christ. Remember him before you "elder" anyone. How many men who have carried the label "elder" would ever mistreat their children the way they have mistreated God's people? Many so-called fathers and mothers do not mistreat, not the way many so-called elders do.

If you do carry the term "elder," and you do treat your children the way you treat some of God's people, you should not be too surprised if your children (and the church). . .rebel.

I hear you saying, "Yes, I am compassionate, and yes, I care; but you do not realize some of the problems we have here. I *had* to say to this brother, 'you straighten up your life or get out.'"

You may look at the office of eldership that way, or you might look at it as an office that is nothing but complete servitude. Of all the people in the church who should strive to exercise authority the *least*, it would be the elders.

"Ah, but I am not an elder, I am a pastor; and these are things which sometimes *must* be done."

Pastor, consider this: There are *priests* in the Roman Catholic church. Their priestly practices grew out of the priestly practices of heathenism. These practices slipped, diluted somewhat, into Protestantism. The Protestant pastor is a revision, a reform, of the Roman Catholic priest. The bone marrow of the clergy continued on even into evangelical Christianity. There is little difference between a priest and a pastor. They are clergy. They are non-laymen, they are special. Unfortunately, in most cases, today's elders are but the grandchildren of this clergical family.

Or, to put it a little less candidly, Luther created the present-day pastoral concept. It is not in the New Testament. It can not be found in *the story*.

Throughout church history, many believers have stepped outside the more traditional practices of the church. Unfortunately, during the last 175 years, most of those who have stepped out, and have then sought to find a more primitive expression of the church, have encountered—or were taught—a strong pervasive eldership, specifically eldership as it was first espoused by John Darby.

Sirs, you who have been recipients of this particular elderology are a clergy. It may be a multiple clergy, but it is still clergy.

If ever we are to break with clergyism, then elders are going to have to be men who are loath to be in leadership.

Elders should be the last resort in incredibly impelling crises. In a perfect world, even then elders would not act.

Who, then, acts in a truly serious situation? That job belongs to an outsider! To the intinerant worker!

This fact—be pleased to know—is one of the most rejected ideas ever presented to the Christian mind.

Nonetheless, you own a New Testament. Start in Acts Chapter One and read forward. Find any crisis in any church, anywhere, that was not resolved by church planters! Not pastors, not elders, but the translocal worker who was most responsible for the existence of the church that is in crisis.

For measuring when elders should act, the situation would have to be worse than the crisis in the church in Thessalonica, worse than the crises in the churches in Galatia, and even worse than the crisis in the church in Corinth. Why? Because in all of those cases the eldership was never called upon. It was the church planter, and only the church planter, who took action.

Once more, you are forced back to the inevitable equation, elders are inseparably linked to the itinerant church planter. Major crises and discipline of God's people . . .are all in his hand. Local life-threatening problems in a local ecclesia are inseparable from a non-local, itinerant church planter. Other problems that arise? They are to get worked out among the brotherhood and sisterhood of the church. Is that possible? Yes. . .if there is a period of time after a church is born, a period of time when there are no designated leaders, when leadership grows up totally in the hands of both the brothers and the sisters.*

*This period of time is so very, very important. One reason: During this period when there are no designated leaders, leaders (of a sort) will arise. Some are elder material and some may be Generalisimo. Let the church planter observe and know the difference.

Rather than lead, men who were workers in Century One encouraged others to lead.

*   *   *

We have now come to the end of eldership as mentioned in the Book of Acts.

Look again at the stage. Who do you see upon it? You see *first* God's people, and you see the church planters. Later, in *some* of the churches, you see elders. But in eight of the nine letters Paul wrote to churches there is no reference to elders or eldership. In all cases where there is a reference to eldership, and there are no exceptions, the elders are irrevocably tied to an itinerant worker. Without that extra-local, non-local, trans-local man, you have no grounds whatsoever for eldership.

As Acts 28 comes to an end, the story told in Acts takes us to the year 61 A.D.—but a great deal happened after 61 A.D. (For instance, Paul wrote seven more books.) There is a great deal which happened, that which is the story, that took place well beyond 61 A.D.

Let us look at Paul's next two letters. . .*and* the setting. Keep a close look out for *today's* eldership.

On with *the story.*

*Y*ou cannot scripturally have elders apart from the itinerant church planter. Do so, if you wish, but do not claim that your philosophy—and your practice—is in any way based on the Word of God. It is not!!

13

Elders in
Colossians and Ephesians

(The events found in these two letters took place after the events
recorded up through Acts 28.)

*A*fter Paul left Ephesus he eventually made his
way to Jerusalem. There was a riot and Paul
ended up in prison in Caesarea.

From Jerusalem he was sent as a prisoner to Rome.
So end the events given us in Acts. But Paul doesn't end
his ministry. Even as a prisoner he continues the work.
He writes four letters to churches while a prisoner in the
imperial city.

Here is the continuing story.

To make this story clear, we must introduce a man
named Epaphras.

Epaphras was from Colossae, a small town situated
about ninety miles east of Ephesus in a land called Asia
Minor. It appears that during the three years Paul was in
Ephesus, Epaphras of Colossae was converted to Christ
while visiting Ephesus. Soon afterwards Epaphras returned
to Colossae. There, in Colossae, a church was born out
of the hands of Epaphras. After perhaps another three
years Epaphras raised up a church in the town of
Hieropolis, and then another in Laodicea.*

Epaphras decided to leave Colossae and travel all the

*Epaphras is, in my judgment, one of the most outstanding figures in
the New Testament.*

way to Rome to visit Paul. (Remember, Paul is a prisoner in Rome, Italy.) The route Epaphras takes carries him up through Greece, to visit the church in Philippi (in northern Greece). The church there fell in love with Epaphras, and Epaphras fell in love with them. After ministering to the Philippians he departed for Rome—by sea—landing at the seaport of Brindisi, and from there Epaphras made his way across Italy and up to Rome. He remained in Rome with Paul for quite a long time. Paul was impressed with Epaphras and with the story of the birth of the church in Colossae, a town he had never seen.

Paul decided to write a letter to the three churches which Epaphras had raised up (Colossae, Hieropolis and Laodicea).

Paul saw Epaphras as a church planter. Later, he even called Epaphras a sent one. . .an apostle.

How old was the church in Colossae when Paul wrote to her? We do not know, perhaps a year old, perhaps two or three. Paul wrote two letters to these three churches. One is called Colossians. The other is *mis*-called *Ephesians*. Actually, that letter was not written to Ephesus but to Colossae, Hieropolis and Laodicea. The two letters were to be read in all three churches.

It is about 62 A.D.

Search those two letters. You will not find a single reference to elders. Not an implication, not a hint. Nothing suggested, nothing between the lines.

When Paul finished those two letters he anticipated that Epaphras would take the letters back to the three churches. Once more you see (1) God's people, and (2) the church planter. . .inseparably linked.

But Epaphras did not take the two letters. He became seriously ill, far too sick to deliver letters to faraway Asia Minor.

Paul did what church planters do. He turned to a young man he had trained and asked him to step in. Now Tychicus was a man Paul had trained for three years in Ephesus. Tychicus was a church planter. (See Acts 20:4, Col. 4:7, Titus 3:12, II Tim. 4:12). It appears that Paul had previously—and later—sent Tychicus out to churches all over the Roman Empire.

God give us the day when ministry comes mostly from *within* the church, and when most of the *help* which churches receive comes from *outside*, and when such help will be mostly from church planters.

Tychicus set out for Asia Minor with those letters in hand. (On his way there, Tychicus—like Epaphras— stopped over at the church in Philippi.)

Tychicus' route was thus: From Rome to Brindisi. From Brindisi a ship to southern Greece. Tychicus then walked to northern Greece and visited the church in Philippi. After visiting the Philippian church, he set sail for Asia Minor, then walked the ninety miles inland to Colossae.

We have a church planter, Paul. We have a church planter, Epaphras. We have a church planter, Tychicus. These are the men who were involved with three churches in eastern Asia Minor. Tychicus remained there for a while, strengthening those three young churches. He then left. This is *the story*!

And what happened to Epaphras? Did he die? No, he lived. And when he was fully recovered, Paul sent Epaphras, not to Colossae, Hieropolis, nor Laodicea, but to Philippi! Epaphras goes to Philippi at Paul's behest, with a letter in his pocket addressed to the ecclesia which gathers in Philippi.

In all of this coming and going and writing of letters and strengthening churches, not one word is written that refers to elders.

Let us now drop in on Philippi. Epaphras is there . . .with a letter to Philippi. Voila! At last, Paul writes a letter to a church and in that letter, for the first time ever, Paul refers to elders. Philippi has elders.

The church in Philippi must be in really, really, great trouble. *Elders* are mentioned. Now we will learn about the place of elders in the church, for sure.

Don't bet the family farm on that idea!

*I*f but the least and frailest, let me be
Evermore numbered with the truly free,
Who find Thy service perfect liberty!

Matthew Pryer

14

At last! Philippi
Does Have Elders!!

*S*ix months pass from the time when Paul wrote his
two letters to Colossae and when he wrote the letter
to the church in Philippi. This is how it all took
place.

When Tychicus left Rome and came to Philippi, he
told the church in Philippi that Epaphras was very ill. The
church in Philippi was disheartened, as they had fallen in
love with Epaphras when he had come to them on his way
from Colossae to Rome. The Philippians then sent a
brother to Rome, to give Paul a gift and to find out if
Epaphras was alive. This brother planned to return home
to Philippi with news of Paul and Epaphras. Paul had a
better idea.

By now Epaphras was fully recovered. Paul seized
upon this situation to write a letter to the church in Philippi
and to send that letter to Philippi by way of *Epaphras*.

Mark this: It is 63 A.D. Paul had raised up the church
in Philippi in the summer of 50 A.D. That means thirteen
years passed between the birth of the church in Philippi
and the time Paul wrote the saints there a letter. In this
letter to the brothers and sisters in Philippi there is, for the

first and only time, the use of the word elders. Once, and only once, to churches.

We do not know when the church in Philippi got elders. Paul was there at least three times. Probably he appointed elders on the third occasion. That means the church in Philippi was at least *nine* years old when it got its elders.

There is one thing that is an absolute certainty. A very strong brotherhood and a very strong sisterhood—you might call it a very strong brethren-ness—had grown up within the church long before elders arrived. And before there were elders? There were the brothers and the sisters! *They* were the ones leading the church. *Always* on the stage of the first century there were two dominant players: (1) the apostles and (2) the Lord's people. Eldership simply cannot take a central role on that stage.

Participation! Participation by so many people, so long, was not overrun by pseudo-clergyism which we know today by the title of eldership.

If a people are the participators of the church, elders are no threat. It is only when we are passive receivers that *any* type of clergy becomes strong. Dictatorial type of eldership is not keen to take over a long standing and strong brotherhood, not without a very concerted effort. Those elders in Philippi came directly out of that brotherhood. Those men were part of that brotherhood. Who they were and what they could do as elders in that church was determined by the wholesale participation of the saints. You cannot expect that people who speak in every meeting and are in on every vital decision will suddenly relinquish this and be overlorded by a few men with whom they got saved, and who, long before they were elders, were simply brothers in the church.

We have neglected looking at the matrix out of which elders come. It is a fatal error.

In our day, when someone in a Bible class does all the talking and everybody else does all the listening, no brotherhood will grow up. And on the day when that teacher starts teaching that "we have to have elders," the people hearing him will nod passively, for passive has been their general state. Soon after, there will be two other men (besides the Bible teacher) elected to be elders. Now you have three people who are called elders who are making great impact into the lives of everyone else (or ruining the lives of everyone).*

That may be the way it is generally done today, but that is not the way it was in Century One. In the first Christian century there was participation by everyone in everything. The first century had no great sit-and-listen mentality. Consequently, all decisions lay with the apostles, the Lord's people and the Holy Spirit. Function belonged to everyone.

Returning to the book of Philippians, there was a long period of time when Philippi did not have anything but those three elements. Rising up out of that soup, that mix, came brothers whom everybody knew *really* well and who never would have become elders in Philippi if they had not been trusted by just about everyone. *These* are the men who became Philippian elders. Their space to

*With the passing of two or three years, someone is bound to get very hurt

input others' lives was extremely limited by the very nature, composition, past history, and experience of the body of Christ in Philippi.

Men become elders (if God's people have real input) who are least likely to run other people's lives.

In every group of Christians, there are always men who would love to run everyone else's lives. (This was also true in the first century.) But over a long period of time, a church comes to understand the dictatorial nature of such men. Let us only hope they discuss that fact before *he* makes *himself* an elder!

A body of people strong in functioning and brotherhood *never* allows such men to become elders.

What really comes out is this: The gentle, the caring, the loving, the quiet, the meek, or at least. . .the *sane*, are usually the men who end up being elders. But only if given enough time! This incubation period precedes the selection of elders. There is an ingredient desperately needed in this mix. It is called *time*. Time when there are *no* local leaders.

Plus. . .

The ingredient of an itinerant church planter.

A long period of time of church life—a period of time long enough for a strong brotherhood to grow up in the church, and an itinerant worker as part of the mixture.

Answer for yourself: Do you believe the elders in Philippi had taken over the direction of the church? Note how much space Paul gave elders in the letter he wrote to the church in Philippi. The elders received one-fourth of one sentence! Do you really believe that *they* are doing virtually all the functioning and the people are sitting and listening?

God's people walking into a meeting, sitting down, being ministered to by elders, and then walking out is not first century. There is no first-century document in existence which points in such a direction. Rather, all the evidence points toward a brotherhood, a sisterhood, a churchhood, *plus* the itinerant church planter.

Paul wrote a total of five letters to churches in major crises (six are spoken to in five letters.) All six churches were in terrible crises—yet no mention of elders. The one letter which Paul wrote to a church and *did* mention elders was the one church that was at peace!

Ironic, is it not? And revealing!

If you will read the last few verses in Philippians you will find that this beautiful church does have a few problems. Who deals with it? Paul doesn't call for the elders to do it; Paul does it himself.

How blessed it is when a church has a problem *internally* and that problem, mercifully, is resolved by someone from the outside.

Once more, *Paul* resolves church crises, *not* elders.

Someone who is on the outside, a foreigner, a stranger to the church comes in? No! The man who personally raised up that church. *That* church planter!

What if the church planter got old and died? If he was worth his salt, he would have left some itinerant church planters to take his place.

Now we come to what has been called the *pastoral* epistles. These *are not* pastoral epistles, as we shall see. These are the three letters in the New Testament that were written *to* church planters *by* a church planter.

**uthority intoxicates**

Samuel Butler

15

Letters to Young Church Planters

*I*t was not until after the Reformation that these three epistles came to be known as the *pastoral* epistles, a result of the fact that the Reformation invented Pastors.

But then, why not call them pastoral epistles; we live in a world where there is little else but pastors on the stage.

In the first century there were church planters. Today, there is a man-invented office called "pastor"...taken from a *verse* in Ephesians. Yet *the story* has no such ubiquitous person as presently carries the title of pastor.

Two of the young men whom Paul raised up and sent out to raise up churches were Titus and Timothy.

When you read the letter called I Timothy, and if you think of Timothy as being young, then be informed that he is at least thirty-two by this time. Chances are he is more like thirty four or perhaps even thirty-six at this time.

Titus grew up in the church in Antioch. He was chosen to go with Paul and Barnabas to Jerusalem to be part of the confrontation which took place there. Titus sat in a room in Jerusalem that contained the twelve original disciples, the Jerusalem elders, Paul and Barnabas, and several others, including Jesus' brother! Titus was a man with a rich heritage. If he was twenty-four when he went to Jerusalem, then at the time Paul wrote to him, Titus would be about thirty-six years of age!

It is to these two men that Paul writes.

Just before we begin looking at these two letters, remember this. These letters were written *by* a church planter.

Consider: From the day of Pentecost onwards, virtually every major piece of literature found in the New Testament was written by a church planter. The only exception to that would be the writings of Luke. And if you will look really carefully at the title page of the book of Acts (written by Luke) you will see that it says "The *Acts* of the Apostles."

Another way to entitle Acts is to call it "*The Deeds of the Church Planters.*"

By the time Paul wrote I Timothy and Titus, there was not a man living, beyond the Twelve and Paul himself (and perhaps Barnabas), with a richer background than Titus.

Titus was present when the church in Antioch was born. He sat under Paul and Barnabas. He met the Twelve in Jerusalem. He *saw* Jerusalem. He visited the gatherings of the ecclesia in Jerusalem, and there he watched that high drama when the Apostles finally decided to bless the work of Barnabas and Paul.

Titus visited the four churches in Galatia. He lived among the three churches in northern Greece. Titus also watched the *birth* of the church in Ephesus in Asia Minor.

He had a great deal to do with helping the church in Corinth out of its mess. When the church in Corinth was an absolute mess, and Paul could not get to Corinth, it was Titus he sent there. He was trained by Paul in Ephesus for three years. Paul then sent Titus out into the smaller cities of Asia Minor *to plant churches!*

Sometime later, Paul sent Titus to the island of *Crete* to plant churches *there.* Then Paul called Titus from Crete and sent another church planter to take Titus' place there.

He is a brother well thought of throughout the whole realm of first century Christendom. *And* he was trained, by Paul, to be a church planter.

You might want to remember this: Titus cross-pollinated with the experiences of brothers from churches in other nations, other cultures, and other provinces. He was not only trained by Paul, but he was trained *with* Timothy, Gaius, Aristarchus, Secundus, Sopater, Tychicus, and Trophimus. He also knew and worked with Epaphras in Asia Minor and also worked with Epaphras in Rome!

That is the man who received the "book of Titus."

This is no incidental brother. Other than Paul of Tarsus, Titus had seen and experienced more than anyone, other than the twelve apostles.

Why does a man who knows the elders in Jerusalem, in Galatia, in Philippi, and Ephesus, and who has known Paul for sixteen or seventeen years, *and* been in the Lord's work for nearly a decade. . .why does he need to be told by Paul what the qualifications of an elder are?

He did not!

Paul (an old man) to explain to Titus (a middle-aged man) what an elder was? Why did Paul bother to tell Titus what an elder was when Titus knew? Why tell him what he already knew?

Ponder that while we look at the two other letters that were written by Paul to yet another young church planter. We will come back to Titus a little later.

Now a close look at another young church planter.

We have made much ado about elders and their qualifications. We have forgotten, however, that what we are reading about elders was written by church planters. We have literally forgotten the place of church planters in the Christian drama. We have certainly given no consideration to how they were trained, what their experiences were, how they were sent out, and their relationship to the local assembly.

When we return to these basic principles, then and then only, is local eldership ever going to make any sense. The planter precedes the elder. The practice of eldership cannot be viable without the return of the church planter.

16

The Man Who Had
Seen and Done Everything!

*W*ho else received a church-planter-to-church-planter letter?

His name was Timothy, and he, like Paul, had been everywhere and seen everything.

Timothy was sitting at the feet of Paul and Barnabas while he was still very young.* And while he was still a young man, he began following Paul and Silas around, watching them plant churches. Timothy watched Paul get beaten up in Philippi. He witnessed the riot in Thessalonica. He watched the birth of the church there. He saw the city of Athens, and later lived for eighteen months in Corinth with Paul. He also travelled with Paul to Ephesus, the first time either he or Paul ever saw that city.

He travelled then with Paul from Greece to Jerusalem and back up to Antioch. He helped prepare for Paul's third church planting journey. For the next four years he lived side by side with Paul in Ephesus and beyond. He once more travelled with Paul to Jerusalem, and saw Paul almost pulled to pieces by a riot. Where he was during Paul's imprisonment in Caesarea, we do not know. But this we do know—later, when Paul was taken to Rome as

Soon after he was converted, as a brand new convert, it was Timothy, more than anyone else, who stood up to the Judaizers who came from Jerusalem to Galatia and tried to have all the Gentiles in Galatia circumcised.

a prisoner, Timothy was by his side.

Timothy visited every church Paul had ever raised up. Like Titus, he had been trained by Paul for three years with Aristarchus, Secundus, Gaius, Sopater, Tychicus, Trophimus.

Timothy was a man who could tell you what the city of Rome was like, as well as Antioch, Athens and Jerusalem.

Keep all that in mind when you read Paul's first letter to Timothy.

That letter was written in 63 A.D. Here is the setting.

Paul was in northern Greece. Timothy was over in Ephesus.

Remember the Ephesian elders?

If you have been taught things about eldership, you have probably been taught that the elders in Ephesus towered over the churches. Men have made a great issue out of the fact that the Ephesians had elders, and not only that they had them, but they see elders running the church. A lot of emphasis is placed on the powerfulness of elders.*

But here is something else that you should remember. Ephesus not only had elders, it had two living, breathing, itinerant church planters "riding herd" on those elders.

As I promised you earlier, get ready for some big shocks.

Look at Chapter 3 of I Timothy. The first thing to be understood is that Paul did not write this chapter for Timothy's benefit. Paul gives a list of the qualifications a person must have to be considered for eldership, yes. But

See our discussion of the Ephesian elders on page 85

Timothy, like Titus, knew all that.

Timothy, like Titus, had met elders in four churches in Galatia and *the* elders in Jerusalem. He knew the elders in Philippi. Timothy had even raised up churches—and perhaps had even ordained elders. Timothy did not need to be told what Paul wrote to him in that letter.

What is going on here?

If Timothy did not need to hear this, why was it written?

Paul was writing these things to Timothy for the sake of those who would read Paul's letter to Timothy. Paul was speaking to the churches through his letter to Timothy. He was letting the churches know what Timothy would be doing, and what Timothy would be looking for in eldership. Paul was giving the Lord's people in Ephesus the who, the what, the where, the when, and the how of eldership.

Paul expected that the church in Ephesus would respond to Timothy. Church planters ordained elders. Obviously, Paul expected both Ephesus (*and* the young churches around Ephesus) and Timothy to respond to these guidelines!

Now go back to Acts 20 and look at Paul's relationship to the elders there in Ephesus.

Consider the fact that, years later, Timothy is in that very same city—Ephesus—when he receives this letter from Paul. There is a church in Ephesus, there are elders there, and on this occasion there is an itinerant church planter visiting Ephesus—Timothy.

Consider the implication!

Let us take all these passages in Acts 20 that men have been using to beat people over the head with, and also this letter to Timothy. Together we get a whole new look at elders.

In chapter 1 Paul is talking about elders/overseers/ watchers. He makes an incredible statement, "It is good for men to desire to be elders."

For starters: Timothy is about to ordain elders in the church in Ephesus. . .a church which *already* has elders!

Wow!

Whatever else this passage in chapter 1 finally tells us, there is one thing that is crystal clear: Eldership is *not* permanent. Reflect on this point for a moment. To be an elder does *not* mean you stay an elder!

Pause for a moment and think about groups you know who have elders. The men selected as elders stay elders for their whole lives (or until the head elder gets disgruntled and removes an elder for disagreeing with him.)

In many cases, these elders begin to feel their importance, and in the process of being administrators and/ or problem solvers, they begin messing up the lives of God's people. Permanent eldership?

There has been meanness, hatefulness, skullduggery, powerplays, back-biting, undermining, splitting of the church and everything else imaginable, by elders *and* by jealous men who were not elders but wanted to be elders so bad that they were salivating for the position.

There are a great many men called elders who believe they are to *stay* elders *forever*, and who are ready at any time to do battle with anyone who looks like he "desires to be an elder."

Ask yourself this question. When a typical, non-traditional church gets elders, just how often do those men usually remain elders?

The answer is usually *always!*

Men stay in this position forever, or until one of those elders crosses the man who is the "super-elder." When the *real leader* feels one of his chosen elders is turning against him, usually there is a fight, an excommunication, or a split—or, more likely, all three. Generally speaking, men remain elders until they either die or cross the real leader.

It goes without saying that elders today are appointed within the fellowship either by a pastor or *someone* who is *local*, and who *remains* local.

If a young man is enthusiastically following a local leader, and the local leader has the young enthusiast elected to eldership so the enthusiast can be controlled by the leader; and if the church, in turn, is controlled by the elders, then you have all the ingredients of a future firestorm. The years pass on. The young enthusiastic elder gets older and wiser. (Some get entrenched, some begin looking at the man who picked him as an elder and begin seeing the true leader through new eyes.) Sometimes what they see is a dictator. A revolt ensues. Carnage follows. Yet this process, as described above, is how most elders get selected.

There should be an atmosphere in the church that

allows virtually any man who fits the very, very general qualifications mentioned in I Timothy to at least be considered as one who can become an elder in the church.

This passage shows us that *becoming* an elder should not cause an upheaval in the church, and *ceasing* to be an elder should not cause an upheaval in the church.

If there is anything this passage implies, it indicates that there is a great deal of movement in the world of eldership. It appears there is *rotation*! The office of eldership is fluid.

If you think that is a shocker, wait until you see what comes as Paul continues to speak to Timothy.

Remember, it was just six years ago that Paul of Tarsus met with the elders of the church in Ephesus. Now, a few years later, there is Paul speaking to Timothy about the possibility of the church in Ephesus getting new elders. Paul has chosen to write this letter to Timothy in such a way that whoever reads the letter, in Ephesus, will know exactly what Paul is saying. Everyone who reads Timothy's letter will be very, very clear about what an elder is *and* who appoints elders, *and* clear that it is good for the church to get *new* elders.

Exactly who did appoint the elders in Ephesus? Paul. And who is going to appoint any new ones? Timothy. (Both men are non-local.) An older church planter is telling a younger church planter that he—Timothy—will be the one who will lay hands on the new elders in the church in Ephesus.

Once more, there is a continuing link between church planter and elder.

Think about it. Those of you who have experienced tragic situations as the consequence of having eldership. What if there had been the teaching that *new* elders should be added? What if someone *outside* that local gathering could have come in and selected new elders, done away with some old elders, or added elders?

Better than that, how wonderful it would be if someone who is not part of the problem could come in from outside the city and guide a church when it has a crisis, any crisis.

God hasten that day!

From a human viewpoint, elders are selected by someone who is not local. Who? The man who planted the church. (Or in this case, the man who planted the church sending another church planter in his place to ordain elders.)

In all the books ever written or all the messages ever spoken which teach eldership—having left out context and timeline—none of these facts are *ever* seen.

Isolated verses begone!

It is Timothy who has fallen heir to the work in Asia Minor. And he certainly had every qualification to be that man. He was present when the church in Ephesus was raised up. He had lived there three years *as a brother*. In the area around Ephesus he had been part of the planting of a number of churches. He had, since then, served long in the area of Asia Minor. Next to Paul, Timothy knew the church in Ephesus best. All that, plus the rest of his rich heritage.

Timothy was now an outsider, called by God. He had

received the blessing of the ecclesia in Lystra to be trained as a church planter. He was trained by Paul.

Note that the man who is going to be dealing with the elders is younger than the very men he is dealing with. No wonder Paul said to Timothy (and the elders read it!): "Let no man despise your youth."

And now, let us turn to I Timothy 5:5-22 and see what else awaits us.

Do you realize that this entire passage is about elders? Most people do not. Do you realize that this entire passage is about the elders in *Ephesus*! Most people do not.

Now, if you will, reread verses 17-22, and then read verse 22.

All this passage is about those *elders* in Ephesus. You know, the elders mentioned in Acts, in a passage that is supposed to *prove* the overlordship of elders!

Read it again! Does this passage change your image of the vaunted, unassailable position of eldership?

Now let us look at the whole passage.

The first thing we learn is that elders are doing what all the other brothers and sisters in the church are doing. The only exception is that they are also preaching and teaching. If they are doing a lot of that, they should get paid. Men who give full time to the ministry should be paid. They should receive money for it. The worker deserves his wages. And yet, Paul, the one who wrote this passage, never took money! Still, he is being very liberal, urging the church to take care of the brother, financially, who ministers.

Verse 19 says that if there is a charge laid against an elder it has to be by two witnesses, otherwise forget it. (That emphasizes that the church can be unhappy with an elder.) Please notice that this principle should hold not only of elders, but of workers, or *anyone* in the church. One charge is no charge at all. Two or three people should be able to say, "This man is running off with the money," or "This man is a dictator," etc.

Now we come to that most mind-boggling of all verses. What if an elder is charged? What if it turns out that he is amiss? (Remember, this is talking about those vaunted, legendary elders in Ephesians who met Paul in Miletus.)

Timothy of Lystra is to bring offending elders before the entire ecclesia in Ephesus!

Timothy.

Elders.

In Ephesus.

In front of the entire church.

Let us go over that again. If an elder is remiss or if he has become amiss, if he has been charged and the charge is found to be true, he is supposed to be disciplined. By whom? The local people? No. By the head elder? No. By the super elder? No. By a pastor? Nope. (You are fifteen hundred years too early for the existence of a today-type pastor.) Then by whom? The elder is to be brought before the entire church. Who is going to bring him there? *The itinerant church planter!*

There it is again.

How much in the history of elders would change if

every man called *elder* knew he could be dragged before the entire ecclesia for not being Christ-like?

Then in verse 21, Paul says to Timothy, "Do not treat one elder nice and another one mean. Don't you be liberal with one and hard on another one. If one of the elders has done a specific thing wrong, he is not to be treated any differently from another elder who has done that same thing wrong. What you do to one, you do the same to all (even to those who give more money!)

"Timothy, you cannot act out of favoritism.

"Furthermore, Timothy, Jesus Christ and the heavenly messengers are watching what you do. Treat one elder the way you do another one."

This is a scary passage.

Elders take note. Are you sure you want to be an elder, first-century style? Many men have written on "discipline in the church," but they seem to overlook disciplining the elders. Paul did not. In fact, he spoke extensively on *discipline* in the church, and only twice did he go so far as to say someone should be brought before the church and rebuked. They were adulterers and elders.

It seems that the elders, more than anyone else, are to be *watched*. The watchers get watched. And if an elder does something he should not do, the itinerant church planter comes in and places him in front of the entire church and then *rebukes* him. Publicly, before the *entire* church.

Place that in your eldership doctrine.

You might also contemplate this question for a moment. If an elder is brought before the church and is rebuked, do you think he would continue on in leadership? Continue just as he had always before? Or might someone else take his place? If he continues as an elder, having been rebuked in front of the whole church, do you think he is going to carry the same image he once did? Perhaps the answer to that is positive; but one thing is for sure, whatever he did wrong, he is not going to do it again!

What is to be learned from this passage? One thing you learn is that an elder is inseparably linked to the itinerant church planter. The second one is: Sir, be careful with your office. God's people are a lot more important than you are. The third thing to be learned?

Probably over 99% of the men who are *called* elders got the title by means unknown to the first-century churches. (Which being interpreted means: You may be *called* an elder, but you are not an elder.)

We are not going to have real eldership nor real elders until we come back to an ancient, long-forgotten ingredient of first-century churches: We must have church planters and they must be non-local and itinerant.

Here are some things we can learn from I Timothy:

• Probably eighty-five per cent of all the men in any church meet the qualifications of an elder as listed in I Timothy.

• Under normal circumstances, a church should wait a long time before it has elders.

• Selection of elders is something that is done frequently, or at least, it is not a once-and-forever matter.

• The addition of elders, and perhaps even the

subtraction of elders, is not infrequent. Perhaps it is even rotational. Let no man stand up and say, "Once an elder, always an elder."

• An elder can get into trouble faster than anybody else in the church! Who watches the watcher? The church does. But also the itinerant church planter does.

• Who lays hands on the new elder? It is not a pastor or any other kind of leader. The first person to lay hands on him is not local. It is the planter of that church or his designate. Perhaps we can add this: Although the people around you may call you an elder, the chances are you are in no way scripturally an elder. By any measurement found in the first century, the possibility that you really are an elder is somewhere between remote, nil, zip and zero.

Now a word to those of you whose toes tingle at the thought that maybe *you* would like to be a church planter. You might want to review the life of Timothy to see what he went through to reach that point.

My dear reader, if you think that eldership is something that demands quality of life, it is not to be compared with what a man must pass through in order to be a church planter.

I urge all men, especially would-be workers, to please read *Overlooked Christianity*. A large part of that book deals with the preparation and training of an itinerant church planter.*

And if you run across a man who calls himself a church

The author plans, someday, to put out a book entitled **The Man Most Needed, but the Man Nobody Wants.** *It is about the desperate need we have in Christendom today to restore the office of the church planter, the itinerant church planter.*

planter, and if he is not at least as qualified as Timothy,** you might want to hold him in reserved suspicion. Or better, run like the dickens!

Now we come to the book of Titus. Folks, things are not going to get any better.

**To clarify what I mean by "at least as qualified as Timothy," please read Overlooked Christianity concerning the kind of training young men should pass through before becoming church planters.

*T*he amount of reliance on authority
measures the amount of decline of religion

Ralph Waldo Emerson

17

The Letter to Titus

*H*ere is a man even more qualified than Timothy to be a church planter.*

Let us look at the setting in which the book of Titus was written. Titus was on the island of Crete when he received this letter from Paul.

The first question that comes up is, "Did Paul plant churches on the island of Crete?" If Paul did, then it would appear that Titus was with him. If Paul did not plant churches in Crete, then it was Titus who planted those churches. Whichever happened, the churches were very much in the Paulinian line of churches. That means that every one of those churches, soon after they were born, were left alone—left without the presence of their church planter. And left alone *before* there were elders in the church. Read the letter carefully and you will see that this is true. There was a lapse of time after Titus raised up the churches there before the question of eldership came up.

Now who is going to choose and ordain elders there on the island of Crete?

We are once again faced with the inevitable. Titus, an itinerant church planter, who was born and raised in

*See Chapter 15

Antioch, Syria and who worked among all the churches in all three of the major land masses where Paul raised up churches*—*this* man Titus is there on the island of Crete. He is going back to the churches on Crete which, until now, have *never* had elders! Paul tells Titus the qualifications of an elder and then tells him to choose and *ordain* elders in the churches on Crete.

Things do not get much clearer than this.

Be assured that Titus (perhaps more than any other man living on the earth in that day except Paul) knew what kind of men to look for in the way of elders. After all, he had met the twelve apostles; he had met the world's first Christian elders (that is, the elders in Jerusalem).

Then why on earth would Paul be telling Titus about qualifications of elders! Because Paul did not write these words so much to Titus, but also for the benefit of those believers on the island of Crete who would read this passage about elders which Paul had written to Titus. The Christians on the island of Crete, after all, had never seen an elder. In this way there would be no question on anyone's part that Titus had Paul's blessing and Paul's spiritual, practical and detailed specifications about the selecting of elders. God's people on Crete knew Titus was on the island of Crete because Paul had sent him there. They also knew Titus would know what he was doing in selecting elders.

To illustrate: If some brother really felt like he should be an elder and Titus did not ordain him to the position, the Lord's people would know that Titus had good reasons for his selection.

Syria, Galatia, western Asia Minor, Greece, Italy. . .and Crete.

Paul was trying to anticipate and intercept any possible problems that would come out of what Titus was doing on Crete at that particular time.

Let us look at these qualifications for consideration of eldership. Don't get drunk. Don't brawl. Don't be exceedingly tied up with money matters or the desire for money. Be a steward. Don't be hot-tempered. *You must not be someone who insists on your own view.* You must be someone who is hospitable, someone who loves good, someone who is sensible, fair-minded and has self-control.

Over half of the Christians I know can fit these qualifications.

But now, let us look at the last one: someone who can answer those who have an opposite opinion.

If you have never experienced church life you may not fully understand what that last comment means.

A church can be having a wonderful experience together with one another and with the Lord, then one day someone who is completely new decides to move into the church. You can be certain that almost every new person coming in has an agenda. That is, he has a view of what a church should be. Here are some views an elder— and a church—might very well meet along the way:

- The church is just relationships, isn't it?
- Why don't we just let Jesus tell us when we should meet together?
- Why do we have church anyway?
- The church is just relationships, isn't it?
- Do we really need a church planter; why can't we do without a church planter?

- I think that the whole reason God created was that we might have relationships.
- The church is just relationships, isn't it?
- I think everybody should speak the truth in love.
- Why do we sing? Why do we have to pray?
- Let's just have little group meetings, and tell one another our problems and our burdens, and then we'll pray for one another. That's what church is.
- The church is just relationships, isn't it?
- Isn't church just counselling? What we really need is a lot of Christian counselling.
- We should rebuke and exhort one another. . .in love.
- The church is friendship. Let's just all spend our time being friends.
- The church is just relationships, isn't it?
- My wife and I will come to the meetings when the Holy Spirit tells us to!
- Why do we have to give money? That's what the organized churches do!
- The church is just relationships, isn't it?

This is the kind of stuff that goes on in *real* church life. These statements usually match the psychological pattern of the person who speaks them.

Then, there is the other side of the coin. You can also be sure that some will see these passages on eldership as saying that elders are in charge. Maybe even very much in charge! These passages are loved and quoted by men who want to control and/or who want to find heretics and burn them (or at least excommunicate them), and in general want to be religious leaders.

It is very good that there be some brothers present in every church who are articulate enough to give some sensible answers to all of the above harebrained notions.

A word about heretics, here, please.

I have been in the ministry for a long time, and I have yet to see anyone walk through the door and come into our midst who is a heretic. I've never met a heretic, *not* within the fellowship of the church. I've never met anyone who did not believe the Bible is the Word of God, not within the church. I have also met a lot of people who want to excommunicate any and everybody who does not agree with their own ideas. Now *these men* have met *a lot* of heretics! Those controlling, dictatorial, overbearing *leaders* have the gift of seeing heretics *everywhere*.

Perhaps the clearest thing that we can understand about an elder, in a real setting of church life, is simply that he is one who can quietly and gently say, "Here is what we are doing. These are the nuts and bolts of what has brought us together. . ." and do this without being pushy or demanding. But who also, having made this statement, understands why the other person feels as he does—*yet stands*. And still stands, even if someone with these questions persists to the point of gathering followers to himself.

What of the qualifications of an elder? Reread the list. This list of qualifications of an elder—as you can see—is not nearly as forbidding as some have made it.

Now let us return to Crete and to Titus.

Remember the setting—not only on the isle of Crete, but the setting throughout the Roman Empire. Things are tense.

Then add this fact: Less that one per cent of the people in the western world could *read*. Only a minuscule number of people could *write*. Ninety-eight per cent of the people of that city lived in poverty, a poverty worse than exists virtually anywhere in the world today. Sickness was rampant. The average life expectancy of a woman was about thirty to thirty-two. The average life expectancy of a man was less than forty.

Point?

The thought of being able to speak clearly and to actually talk for over two minutes to a gathering of people was something that never even crossed the minds of most people. Keeping this setting in mind helps us better understand these passages about *ministry*. Few in *any* first-century church had the ability to do what we call "public speaking."

There is another passage in Titus that demands our attention (Titus 3:12). This passage once more shows us how closely eldership is tied to the itinerant church planter. And not only the elder, but also the church herself is tied to that travelling worker. This passage opens up for us a world of which present-day Christianity knows virtually nothing.

Paul now tells Titus, after ordaining elders in the churches: "Leave! Leave Crete and come back to Asia Minor." Specifically, Paul tells Titus to come to the town of Nicopolis, a town not far from Ephesus. That means that Crete will not have a travelling worker.

Or does it?

Paul says to Titus, "Leave Crete and come to me, Titus." Then he adds, "I am sending another brother to take your place!"

Who is the one who is going to take Titus' place? Someone who will next travel across the island of Crete, encouraging the churches?

Paul has not made up his mind yet. It will either be Tychicus or a brother named Artemas. (We have no idea who Artemas is. But we surely, surely know who *Tychicus* is.)

Tychicus

You might want to study Tychicus' life. In so doing you will see just how well-equipped he is to take over for Titus. You will see what brother Tychicus has gone through to bring him to the point where he would be called on to go to Crete.

Note that Tychicus is one of those men whom Paul has trained. . .to be a church planter. And who is Artemas? He seems to belong to an emerging new group of workers, a fifth generation of church planters. (Please see *Overlooked Christianity*.) It is Paul, the itinerant worker, who sent Titus, the itinerant worker, to Crete. Now it is also Paul, the itinerant worker, who is calling Titus, the itinerant worker, to leave Crete. It is Paul, the itinerant worker, who is sending either Artemas or Tychicus to take the place of Titus.

There is a point here.

These men move around!

We simply have no such counterpart in our age. That loss is incalculable!

They do not stay in one place. Nor is this an isolated scene. Paul is sending men out all over the Roman Empire and also asking them to leave wherever they are and go somewhere else. These men are in the business of (1) raising up churches and (2) strengthening the churches. This is a first-century element critical to that day but lost in our day.

Yet, in all that was going on in the first century, in the minds of God's people eldership existed only in relationship to these itinerant men. You can go a little further and say that the same was true of the churches. In Century One, the church was inseparably linked to men who were not around a whole lot.

Dear reader, you will never have eldership as it should be when the most influential person in a church is someone *local*. The most influential person in a church is *not in* that church! If the most influential person in the church is *in* the church, that church is courting disaster.

Dear local brother in a place of leadership, you can never adequately resolve the crucial problems which the church you belong to is presently going through. . .nor those crises which it will pass through in the future. The reason is simple. You are local. Being local means you are therefore part of the problem. The only way you are going to deal with a local problem when you yourself are local is to do something unwise or unacceptable to many who are present.

You have no long term way of resolving problems. In very bad situations an outside worker, closely involved in that church, is your only hope.

Oh yes, there is one alternative. You can refuse to do anything to correct the problem. But remember, the church is therefore going to splinter, split, divide, collapse, or—just as likely—die a long, slow, agonizing death. These are exactly the same things which will happen if you *do* take action!

There is no good way to deal with crises when *everyone* is local. Not in church life, first-century style.

The continuing wholesomeness and health of a church is inexorably tied to the church planter who is (or should be) non local—a man who really has no vested local interest. Interested in the church, yes. Compassion for the church, yes. Patient beyond measure, yes. Understanding toward all, yes. Burdened for the church, yes. But not someone who finds the very purpose and meaning of his life tied up in being a local leader.

We close the book of Titus, and in so doing, close all that Paul wrote about elders. But just before we do, let us look at the results of today's Christianity not having church planters. Non-local church planters. Look at. . .

*T*he triumph of demagogies is short-lived.
But the ruins are eternal.

Peguy

18

The Price We Are Paying

*W*e are paying a terrible price for having lost the office of church planter, perhaps greater than we realize.

Today, as we read the Scripture—we literally have to ignore his existence. That is a large hunk of Scripture! The result of ignoring this office? Whatever we do, without the church planter we have no alternative except to be *un*scriptural. That, in turn, forces us to be totally dishonest in our use of the Word of God.

We have, for instance, substituted the pastor in place of the church planter. Take a closer look at such a foolish act! First, the pastor is local. Second, the pastor—as we know him—did not exist in New Testament times. He is a concoction of history. You can never find this apparition in the story.

This one fact is enough to show us all how far off the church is from first-century reality.

In Scripture, elders are inseperably linked with the church planter. We do not have church planters, so we must either invent pastors to take their places, or create elders who are, basically, a *plurality* of clergy. Whatever we do, we kill functioning. We preserve clergy, God's people sit and listen, and functioning of the body is never experienced.

Most of Acts is about the deeds of church planters. We do not have church planters, so we lose half of Acts. That is not all. With such a vast loss, we have invented two types of people to take the church planter's place! Here at home, we have pastors. (Pastors are not in the story!) Those who are sent out are called missionaries! (For example, we say Paul's three *"missionary* journeys." But Paul was not a missionary. Paul is a model of how churches are to be raised up locally, nationally, internationally. By making Paul a "foreign" missionary, we then do things differently "on the foreign field" from the way we do things here at home. By this reasoning we get to skip nine-tenths of *the story*.

After seventeen hundred years of random evolving we have ended up with a "back here at home" kind of church, while seeing a *mission field* church as something different from "back home". Paul is a model for all workers and all churches everywhere.

In this ethereal invention of "church," we get to have church buildings, pastors, pulpit, pews, elders appointed by committees, or—in the less formal type churches— elders selected by the Bible teacher or a man who is leading a fellowship of believers into the selection of elders (elders who agree with him).

We have ended up with a non-new-testament New Testament! With a Christianity that is vaguely related to the New Testament, yet all the while. . .*we still manage to see them* in the New Testament. We end up living in a non-Scriptural fantasyland, and while standing in the midst of the fantasyland you find us crying out: "Let us obey the Word of God and be 100% faithful to it!"

That, dear reader, is fantasyland indeed.

It would help a great deal if we would, before we do anything else, find and learn *the story.*

God deliver us back to the story. Give us back our church planters, and the Paulinian way of church life.

WHAT WE HAVE LEARNED SO FAR

As we leave Paul's letters and move on to later books of the New Testament, what have we discovered so far?

First, let us hope this will cause men to loosen their grip on today's teachings about elders. It is also hoped that, having seen this much of *the story,* it might help us understand there is another way to find out what is going on in the New Testament other than plucking verses out of context and calling the results "New Testament teachings."

Perhaps we have seen that John Darby was amiss in the way he taught and bequeathed eldership to evangelical Christianity. Darby's sons and grandsons (and cousins and nephews) have not helped us see a true picture of church life.

You who have made eldership so strong, it may be that you have made it too strong.

As for that Bible class you belong to, it is not a church. The genuine experience of church life has been fairly rare throughout church history. It is distinctly possible that that which is called "church" is not a church, and those men who are elders are not—at least not first-century style.

*   *   *

We come now to the remaining peeks the New Testament gives us into eldership. We will continue to follow the chronological order and we will continue to look at these passages in their total context.

*V*irtually everything we are taught about the New Testament, theology and Bible teachings comes from our *use* of the Bible, rather than from the Bible.

19

I & II Peter
and
Hebrews

*S*hall we look first at Hebrews, or I Peter? Interestingly enough, Peter's first letter was written before the book of Hebrews.

Let us begin, therefore, with Peter's first letter. But before we start quoting anything in this letter about elders, we would be wise to know the circumstances in which I Peter and Hebrews were written.

Paul's last letter (II Timothy) and Peter's letters have a great deal in common, in that there is reflected in these letters a foreboding atmosphere among Christians all over the Roman Empire. A sense of dread, of impending disaster surrounds the work of God throughout the empire.

This first letter Peter penned was probably written around 65 A.D. Paul's second letter to Timothy was probably written around 67 A.D. These are troubled years indeed. Neither man has long to live.

The setting of the book of Hebrews is not easy to know. Chances are it was written around 69 A.D., not too long before the fall and destruction of Jerusalem.

Suffice it to say a deluge of persecution awaits the churches all over the empire. Dark days are growing darker. Fears, it turned out, were justified.

There was growing unrest in Jerusalem and in all Israel. Throughout Israel there is talk of rebellion against Rome. Among Jews, there is a strong teaching afoot: *"If we rebel against Rome, the Messiah will come. He will deliver us from the emperor. He will overthrow the Roman Empire. He is but waiting for us to act."*

Peter knew that if Rome did invade Israel in great force, the Christians *would* flee. Jesus' teachings on what to do if Rome's army comes were all too clear. The question was, where would Jewish Christians flee to? Peter might have chuckled at the thought, or he might have been embarrassed at the thought, but there is no question that he knew the answer to that question.

Jewish Christians in Jerusalem, Judea and Galilee would flee north into cities with *gentile* churches. In fact, fleeing Jews would end up in the churches *Paul* had planted.

How ironic!

That is, Paul (or the eight young men whom he trained to take his place) had planted the churches the Jews would flee to. In just about any area, Jews going north would became part of gatherings planted by the ever-controversial Paul. Even Rome, if they fled as far as Rome. Or Crete!

After the fall and destruction of Jerusalem, most of the Jewish people did flee north, and they did end up becoming part of Paulinian churches.

Isn't that incredible: The outcast won!

Whoever wrote the book of Hebrews wrote with this scenario as his backdrop. He was anticipating what was to come in the way of problems. There is a possibility that Hebrews was written even as the armies of Rome were setting sail to march against Israel and to lay Jerusalem to waste.

With this scene in mind (*Christian* Jews about to flee from a Roman invasion and about to become a part of the Gentile world), let us read the passage that Peter writes about *elders*. Peter is speaking as an old man and speaking to those people who are used to the elders in Judea.

(I am an elder, you are elders; I am appealing to you, as elders.)

Peter then makes an impassioned plea for elders *not* to lord it over the Lord's people. Put it another way. Peter asks them to set an example: Do not be dictators. That would mean to set an example of patience, compassion, and forbearing.

Is Peter's eye on Jewish elders, or Gentile elders? Or both?

Who does Peter give as an example for elders to imitate? To all elders, Peter presents Jesus Christ. He says to those elders, think about the Great Shepherd. The elder named Peter goes on to say:

As sure as I will share the glory with the Lord when He returns, so will you if you have cared for the flock of God. If you have been a good watcher, and if you have watched willingly and not just because you were getting paid to watch. You are servants. But you are not serving men. You are serving God. Keep that in mind.

What Peter had to say to these elders can be summed

up in this: *Lead by example. Have compassion and care for the church of Jesus Christ. Imitate Jesus Christ. And don't forget that God is watching you.*

Peter then speaks to those who are not elders, especially to young men. He asks them to defer to the older men.

Peter stops, considers his words, and decides to balance what he has said. He breaks into one of the strongest appeals for humility that is found in the New Testament. He says to the church, you be what elders are. It is almost as if Peter is telling everyone to be an elder. Be on guard, and watch out for one another and one another's needs.

Dear reader! Dear brothers and sisters, what a passage for a church to reach for.

The churches Peter wrote to there in Galilee and Judea were mature. It had been 34 years since Pentecost. Yet these churches—and those elders—still ran the danger of *tradition* and of keeping to their own little world, i.e. conserving what is, and not changing what needs to be changed.

The danger of stagnation is another good reason why a church should go to great lengths to bring in new elders from time to time. Perhaps also to even dare to ask some of the other brothers who are elders to step down. It also shows the desperate need all churches have of developing a strong brotherhood. Every church needs a strong reservoir of leadership material, one larger than the tiny universe of elders. But the present-day focus of leadership of a church being the franchise of elders prevents a larger pool of leadership from developing.

Finally, stagnation of eldership only highlights the fact that we need restless workers; there needs to be, there *must* always be, a tension between local conservatism and the non-local worker with a world view.

The man who wrote this letter was an *itinerant church planter* and fitted very well into that category.

Peter, the chief apostle, is drawing up the conditions and laying down the parameters. He is not your Bible teacher, and he is not your pastor, and he is not some local super-elder. Peter is an old man who has travelled all over the Roman Empire. He is a church planter. He is an extra-local worker who has played a part in the selection and ordination of the very elders who are reading his letter.

If Peter did not personally play a role in selecting some of the Jerusalem elders, then John did. Or James or Thomas or Matthew.

When you quote the New Testament, be careful. The chances are about twenty-five to two that you are quoting a church planter. (You could make that twenty-six to one, because Acts records what church planters do.)* That pretty well means all those verses you held in your hand which might be used to prove an all-encompassing eldership have been taken away from you. . .by church planters who selected the elders and who wrote those letters you are quoting!

Peter's words were strong. They were firm. One of the greatest flaws in modern day teaching of eldership is that elders are not responsible to anyone except God (or a pastor). If you are an elder and you are responsible to someone, chances are the man you are responsible to

---

Of the twenty-seven books in the New Testament, only Acts and Luke appear to be written by someone who is not a church planter.

probably invented a church structure that made him in charge and made *you* responsible to him.

Look around. Do you have an itinerant worker? Where did he come from and what are his qualifications? Again, I would ask you to read *Overlooked Christianity** for answers to that question.

Every elder mentioned in the New Testament had to report to a church planter. The watchers were being watched (1) by compassionate and broken men who themselves were not local, and (2) by God's people. . .who were part of a strong brotherhood and sisterhood.

Once more we face the inexorable link.

To paraphrase the Chinese laundryman who said "You gottee no tickee, you gettee no laundry": "You gottee no church planters, then you gottee no elders."

Let us hope that both the Jewish and Gentile elders read Peter's letter. Both would need to remember Peter's words after the Jews fled Israel. So would those circumcized young men who probably found themselves in churches with uncircumcized elders!

We now come to the book of Hebrews.

And someday, perhaps, a book entitled **The Man Nobody Wants.**

"The real crisis today is not between Catholics and Protestants but between traditional and *experimental* church life."

Harvey Cox
Secular City
1966

20

Hebrews

ho wrote Hebrews nobody knows. Probably not Paul, for he was almost certainly dead before this book was written.

Early tradition says Hebrews was written by Barnabas. I hope so, for he was a man who lived and breathed compassion.

It is that brutal passage in Hebrews (13:17) which awaits our attention. This one isolated sentence has been the slaughtering tool used against so many innocent people by men justifying their conduct as elders. This passage is quoted as being a reference to elders or shepherds. It is not.

This passage of Scripture is in reference to church planters, not elders.

Hebrews was written to churches in Israel, churches about to undergo great persecution. There was an excellent chance that, as a nation, Israel would be destroyed. Jesus had predicted the end of Jerusalem, and had told His followers to flee quickly when they saw Jerusalem surrounded by foreign soldiers.

That meant most Jewish Christians would have to flee

to the Gentile world. Specifically that meant Jewish Christians would find themselves in Gentile churches in a Gentile world. But that was not all.

Jews were going to be faced with working with Gentile church planters!

Jews gathering in Gentile churches would discover these churches *already* had elders, Gentile elders. Gentile believers, Gentile elders, Gentile workers who had not come from the ministry of the Twelve.

This is an impossible thought to lay hold of.

Reread Hebrews 13:17 in the light *of this*. What you are reading is an appeal by the author to the Jewish believers to respect the situation in which they find themselves when they gather in the churches in other lands. Why write these words? The thought of being in a Gentile church and going along with *their* ways was not an idea appealing to most Jews, to say the very least that can be said.

Perhaps the worst part was that the fleeing Jews were going to have to work with travelling Gentile church planters. That would be difficult. The writer of Hebrews appeals to the Jews to respect those *uncircumcized* workers.

*   *   *

Move down the page just a little, and you will once again find that inexorable link between the travelling church planter and the local church.

To see this more clearly, let us imagine that it was Barnabas who wrote this letter.

Listen to what Barnabas says. Timothy has been in jail, and now he is out. Timothy (now in his forties) is a *Gentile* church worker. We are seeing Jewish churches being informed about the welfare of a *Gentile* worker. The Jewish churches *and* the Gentile churches have been drawn closer together in this world crisis of persecution.

The writer of this book then says, "I am coming to visit you." The author is a worker who travels. Now note this: The author is Jewish, writing to Jewish churches, but he hopes he will have *Timothy*, a church planter—a *Gentile* church planter—with him when he arrives.

A Gentile worker, with a Jewish worker—travelling to Jewish churches! The mind of the church, in Century One, was that of receiving outside workers, though infrequently. This was a thought common to both Jewish churches and Gentile churches.

Elders receive *no* comment in this book. The epistles, on the other hand, are knee deep in references to extra-local workers. God haste the day we get back to this mind, and stop investing non-Scriptural ways and non-Scriptural people, to get around the absence of the itinerant church planter.

There is one other book in the New Testament which mentions elders. (We have no idea when it was written, and only a guess at who wrote it.) Let us go to the book of. . .

*F*ind one verse in all the New Testament which remotely implies that the role of the church planter is supposed to fall to anyone else. The role of church planter remains that of the itinerant church planter. . .or the itinerant church planter who takes his place!

21

The Book of James

*N*obody knows who wrote James, or why or where or to whom.

James makes *one* reference to elders. In so doing he gives us the clearest insight into the practical practice of eldership.

When you are sick, call for the elders, to pray, to anoint.

To those of you who are very strong on elders playing a directive role in the life of God's people, please look at how the writer of this letter words his sentence. This is the kind of unconscious remarks one makes which can, nonetheless, reveal to us the surrounding matrix in which he lives and the way he thinks and conceptualizes.

When one is sick, let *him* call the elders.

The elder does not come unless invited. The amount of role an elder plays in another person's life is, to some extent, limited primarily by *that* person, *not* the elders. (There are exceptions, such as immorality and the like.) Elders pray for the ill in the church. We come now to a book that has innumerable references to elders, *and* no references at all. We come to:

The Book of
REVELATION

You will find the word elder mentioned over and again in the book of Revelation. Be a little careful before you quote *any* of those verses. All references to elders in Revelation are references to elders *in heaven*. Not one of these refers to an elder on this earth.

Lastly, just to remind you—the book of Revelation was written by John, who had lived his life as a *travelling church planter*. *He*, not elders, is dealing with local church problems. There is a pattern here, dear reader, a pattern lost to us.

*   *   *

Now we must ask ourselves: In the light of what we have seen, what should we expect elders to be and what should we expect of eldership?

22

Then What is an Elder?

*W*hat are we looking for in eldership, two millenniums later?

From Scripture can we *really* find a clear picture of elders?

• Some churches had elders, some did not. Let us stay with that practice.

• Of those churches which did have elders, some of these churches were given elders (at the instigation of church planters and the Holy Spirit) not long after the church began. . .but *never* without a lapse of time when there were no leaders present, never. (Not even a home Bible teacher.) On the other hand, some churches did not receive elders until long after their birth. Remember, some churches *never* had elders.

• All eldership in a local assembly was closely associated with an outside worker, a church planter.

• Churches in crises looked to the outside—to travelling, itinerant church planters. They did *not* look to local elders to resolve crises.

In all the crises in all the churches that Paul planted,

there is not one time ever when Paul called on local elders to step in. The crisis had only two resolving elements (1) God's people and (2) the non-local church planter.

- Elders pray for the sick.
- Elders watch, non-local workers *act.*
- Elders answer to (1) God's people and (2) the non-local worker.
- Elders are to be the soul of discretion and patience . . .literally a buffer to those in the church who are *not* patient with others.
- Eldership is fluid—churches get new elders from time to time. Others stop being elders.
- The choice of new elders is at the discretion of the non-local worker.
- Wayward elders (and adulterers) are to be brought before the church and publically rebuked!

Which raises an obvious question: What do we do? We have no itinerant church planters!

That brings us to look at some very disturbing facts about all that has come into existence *because* of the absence of church planters. A lot of what has arisen *instead,* to take the place of church planters, could scare Halloween.

As we now see.

hen we bought into a dispensationalism which dispensed with the role of the itinerant church planter, we destroyed any and all truly honest ways to follow New Testament teachings. The itinerant church planter singly plays too large a role in the first-century story for him to be removed. There is no "New Testament Christianity" without him. And there is certainly no New Testament teaching that says his office is to be voided, nor is there any hint of who would take his duties if he were to be removed from the scene.

23

Missing Persons

*U*ntil the return of the itinerant worker we really have no way to be scriptural when it comes to church life. This certainly includes elders.

A return to experiential church life is our first and greatest problem to solve. Without the church planter—this lost office—we are only thrashing about in the dark. We have invented substitutes right and left. We are presently filled with indefensible practices. In the absence of the keystone to church life, the present practice of Christianity will only breed more non-Scriptural children. Remove the church planter and you *cannot* have a church . . .first-century style.

To illustrate.

Let us say there is a group of believers meeting in a home. These brothers and sisters are very close-knit. Suddenly comes the devastating news that there has been, or is, immorality in the group.

You go to the New Testament and start trying to find teaching on church discipline.

This is the way it will probably go:

"It says it here in the Bible. . .so let us do *that*. We must be obeying the Word!"

We are so conditioned to approach Scripture this way that it is virtually impossible to break through this mindset.

No one seems to have noted that from Pentecost on, you will find no situations involving church discipline except it is handled by (1) the non-local worker, and (2) God's people. This simple fact cannot be found in Scripture. Oh, it *is* in Scripture, but we cannot find it. Now, that is serious. When something is in the Bible and we cannot find it. That is but one small example of how the evangelical mind can look at Scripture and *not* see the obvious.

As you read those discipline-them-this-way Scriptures, also remember who wrote these words. It is a "not-local" brother, and he is giving instruction to a church—not a Bible class. And this extra-local man is getting very much involved locally.

Nothing like that exists today. We long ago stopped having these non-local men who burned for the expression of the local assemblies throughout the world. Some generation, a long time ago, gave up on the central need of having *churches planted* the way churches had been planted in Century One. Let us look for the return of the church planter. But let us pray that when they return they will do so first-century style and with first-century stature, patience and integrity.

We have no present-day concept of churches being raised in the way they were raised up in Century One. It is, to say the least, a lost art. The raising up of non-local workers is also a lost art, in desperate need of restoration. Consider, do you know of or have you heard of churches being brought into existence by a non-local Christian worker who, soon after the church is born, up and leaves? It is simply an incongruous concept. Yet any other approach to church life is scripturally untenable and is courting a nonscriptural disaster. And it is impossible to properly deal with church crises in a scriptural way when *everything* came into existence in a nonscriptural manner. This includes elders!

Is there a solution?

Not really!

In fact, this book is of little value to most Christians and virtually all churches presently constructed as they are.

This book may help many to see the folly of present eldership. It may help take a bite out of the "shepherding" teaching and the "submission and authority" movement. At least, it may help many who are caught in these groups to head for the door.

But most of what is in this book needs a totally new habitat. This book will not help those in the episcopal structure, such as the Catholic church or Anglican church.

It will not help Lutherans, Presbyterians, and Methodists.

Nor will it aid Baptists, Pentecostals, and independent churches.

Neither will it help para-church organizations—most of which are episcopal in structure (that is, all things come from the top down, eventually reaching those at the bottom who have been taught to *obey* those at the top).

Let us hope it helps those in Bible classes, house churches, and assorted other Christian groups outside the traditional churches which are strong on eldership.

But a fifth kind of church is needed—the organic church. A whole new way—a radically new church expression—unique to anything now on this planet. A church expression not yet born.

Church life for those who are living in hard times with something going on called "church," but who really want the ecclesia: To *you* this book is penned.

This book belongs to the future. *You* are that future.

Further, it will take a new breed of workers and a new generation of believers willing to do things in a wholly different way. It is also for you, a future generation of workers, that this book is penned.

Now, a question.

A question for those who teach a strong eldership, submission and authority, covering, and shepherding.

24

A Question

*I*t is often heard in our day, "Touch not the Lord's anointed." It is also often heard, "Submit to those whom God has placed over you."

Here is the question. Pray tell, *when* did *God* make those men *His* anointed? Just when did God place men in authority over God's people? When were *you* given authority, by God himself, over others? Was it after you went through a discipleship training course? (The course lasted six weeks? Three months? *Six* months?)

Or was it when you started a Bible class in your home? When was it God anointed you? Just when did God place you in authority over your Bible class attendees? Were you shaving? Changing a tire? Sleeping? Eating a pizza?

You started a church (or you joined a para-church organization). You went through their discipling training class. After you finished this training, someone assigned twenty young people to you to train. Just when in this process did you become the Lord's anointed? When did *God* place you in authority over. . .anyone?

It is a sign of deep internal weakness and first magnitude insecurity on your part to even quote these verses at someone. These words belong in the church, for the church, to the church, and in the context of church life experience, first-century style. Not a Bible class. Not a para-church organization. Not a "go to church on Sunday morning" kind of church.

We have a long way to go before we dare club God's people with these sentence fragments!

We saw in the previous chapter four types of churches that are abroad in the land today: hierarchial, reform and episcopal, congregational, and para-church organizations.

**Again
A fifth kind of church is needed
—a totally new and different
expression of church life**

Some day there must be—there will be—an expression of the church, a people and workers, who reflect a wholly different matrix and outlook.

I have sought to speak to believers who are part of those *other* four types of church expression about the need of a new expression of church life. Communication on this subject is difficult.

In a way, this book does not really end here. In writing it, I wanted to include much more about an organic church. And words to *future generations*.

In the meantime, here is—at the very least—a lighthouse showing you the direction to a better way than what is about in the land today.

For a few, perhaps you will reconsider what you are doing and head for higher ground, ground that was trod by the ancients, yet not often tried since. A change into uncharted places and to breathtaking adventure.

A Closing Word

Remember one thing, above all else, which you have found in this book.

There is a far better and far more accurate way to learn what the New Testament says than through employing isolated proof text!

Revolutionary Books for Revolutionary-minded Christians

Books You Might Like To Read

◆ **Radical Books for Radical Readers**

BEYOND RADICAL

A simple, historical introduction into how we got all of our present-day practices.

You will be thunderstruck to discover that there is really nothing we are doing today that came directly out of man's determination to be scriptural. Virtually everything we do came into being sometime during church history, after the New Testament. We have spent the rest of our time trying to bend the Scripture to justify the practice.

WHEN THE CHURCH WAS LED ONLY BY LAYMEN

The word *elder* appears in the New Testament seventeen times, the word *pastor* appears only once (and nobody knows what that word had reference to, because there is no place in the first-century story in which he is clearly seen).

But there are over one hundred and thirty references from the day of Pentecost forward that refer to either "brothers" or "brothers and the sisters." (Greek: *Adolphus*). *These* were the people who were leading the church. There are only two major players, from a human viewpoint, upon the first-century stage. They are the church planters and God's people—the brothers and the sisters. Everything else is a footnote.

OVERLOOKED CHRISTIANITY

What is the view of the Trinity on these three critical aspects of faith:

1) How to live the Christian life

2) What is "church" really supposed to look like

3) How are workers—specifically *church* planters—supposed to be trained

Revolutionary, radical and arresting! These are the words which best describe this one-of-a-kind book! *Overlooked Christianity* makes a great companion book to *Rethinking Elders* and gives clear answers about *what to do*!

AN OPEN LETTER TO
HOUSE CHURCH LEADERS

A simple statement on what it is a more primitive expression of the Christian faith should be centering on.

◆ **Books which show what the Christian faith was like "first-century style"**

REVOLUTION
THE SILAS DIARY
THE TITUS DIARY

The story! Perhaps the best way we will ever understand what it was like from the day of Pentecost in 30 A.D. until the close of the first century is simply to know the story. Allow yourself to be treated to, and enthralled by, that story. (Warning: Knowing the story will change your life forever.) You will find that story in every detail, with nothing missing, in these three books.

◆ **Books which glorify Jesus Christ**

> ### THE DIVINE ROMANCE
> A book of awe, wonder and beauty.

> ### THE CHRONICLES OF THE DOOR:
> The record of heaven;
> **THE BEGINNING**
> **THE ESCAPE**
> **THE BIRTH**
> **THE TRIUMPH (the resurrection)**
> **THE RETURN**

◆ **Books which show you how to experience Christ**

These following books serve as an introduction to the Deeper Christian Life:

LIVING BY THE HIGHEST LIFE
THE SECRET TO THE CHRISTIAN LIFE
THE INWARD JOURNEY

◆ **Books that Heal**

Here are books that have been used all over the world, and in many languages, to heal Christians from the deep, deep pains they experience as they go through life. Some were written for Christians who have been damaged by their churches and damaged by other Christians. Others are books which help you understand the ways of God as they are now working in your life. All of these books are known and loved around the world.

A TALE OF THREE KINGS

A study in brokenness.

THE PRISONER IN THE THIRD CELL

A study in the mysteries of God's ways, especially when He works contrary to all your understanding and expectations of Him

CRUCIFIED BY CHRISTIANS

Healing for Christians who have been crucified by other Christians.

Contact SeedSowers Publishing House for a catalog of these and other books, including great classics on the deeper Christian life, as well as new publications that will be appearing annually.

SeedSowers Publishing House

Books by Gene Edwards

Overlooked Christianity
Rethinking Elders
The Silas Diary
Beyond Radical.
When the Church Was Led Only By Laymen
An Open Letter To House Church Leaders
Crucified by Christians
The Highest Life
The Secret to the Christian Life
The Inward Journey
The Prisoner in the Third Cell
A Tale of Three Kings
How To Meet Under the Headship of Jesus Christ
The Divine Romance
Letters to a Devastated Christian
Revolution! *The Story of the Early Church*
Climb the Highest Mountain
The Chronicles of the Door:

> The Beginning
> The Escape
> The Birth.
> The Triumph
> The Return

Books by Jeanne Guyon

Experiencing the Depths of Jesus Christ
Union with God
Spiritual Torrents
Final Steps in Christian Maturity
Song of the Bride
Guyon Speaks Again

Great Books By Other Authors

Bone of His Bone *(F. J. Huegel)*
The House of God *(T. Austin Sparks) Paperback*
The Centrality of Christ *(Sparks) Paperback*
Christ as All in All *(Haller)*
The Key to Triumphant Living *(Taylor)*
Which Being Interpreted Means *(Taylor)*
The Open Church *(Rutz)*
The Seeking Heart *(Fenelon)*
Beholding and Becoming *(Coulter)*
Church Unity *(Nee, Litzman, Edwards)*
Let's Return to Christian Unity *(Kurosaki)*
You Can Witness With Confidence *(Rinker)*
Turkeys and Eagles *(Peter Lord)*
Going to Church in the First Century *(Banks)*
When The Church Was Young *(Loosley)*
The Passing of the Torch *(Chen)*
Practicing His Presence *(Lawrence, Laubach)*
The Spiritual Guide *(Molinos)*
Torch of the Testimony *(Kennedy)*
Church Life Before Constantine *(Snyder)*
The Ultimate Intention *(Fromke)*

Please call for prices.

The SeedSowers
P.O. Box 285
Sargent, GA 30275
800-645-2342